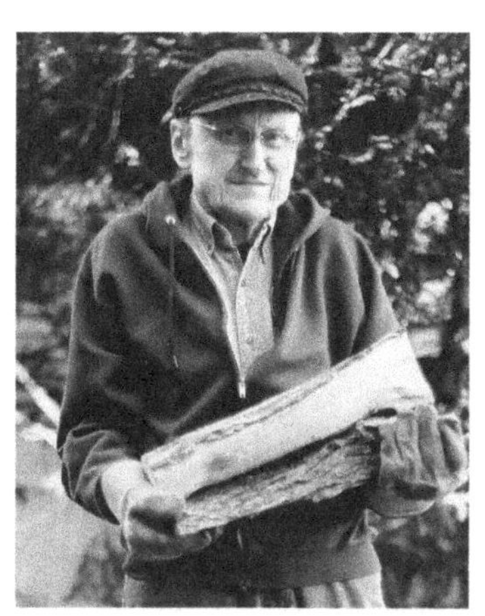

With love
that covers
a lot of
years &
miles

Bill

WILLIAM ZANDER

Poems
Story
Drawings
Photographs
Memories

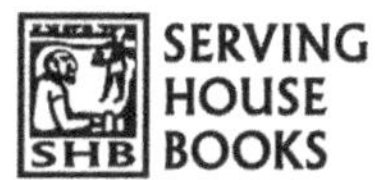

SERVING HOUSE BOOKS

William Zander: Poems, Drawings, Photographs, Memories

Copyright © Estate of William Zander, 2019

ISBN: 978-1-947175-17-4

Library of Congress Control Number: 2019946466

Cover drawing by William Zander

Serving House Books logo by Barry Lereng Wilmont

Published by Serving House Books

Copenhagen, Denmark and Florham Park, NJ

www.servinghousebooks.com

Member of The Independent Book Publishers Association

First Serving House Books Edition 2019

Prepared by Alison and Walter Cummins, Alex Zander, and Renée Ashley.
Thanks to Jeffrey Triggs for helping select the poems to include.

WILLIAM ZANDER

William "Bill" Zander — the quotation marks were intentional irony — possessed unusual talents. Most publicly, his creative strengths were revealed in more than one hundred published poems and in two books — *Distances* and *Gone Haywire* — and a chapbook — *Winter Trees*. He also wrote reviews, fiction, feature stories, and nature articles.

His drawing skills will come as a happy surprise to many who knew him, the sketch books and impromptu placemats shown only to family and friends. After cartoons in his college humor magazine and a gag greeting card released during the short time he worked for Hallmark, he never submitted his artwork. Drawing was essentially a private pleasure.

Bill, with extensive musical knowledge, played guitar and wrote jokey songs, like "Going to New Jersey Blues" and "Does Your Mother Know You're Sleeping with a Hippie?"

Fishing was a passion, hours spent with a flyrod on streams or in a boat anchored in the middle of a lake. After the season, he tied flies with careful precision. Research and accuracy were central to Bill in all of his activities, including his years of teaching.

Anyone who spent just minutes in Bill's company knew how inventively funny he could be, clever with words and zany in action. But that was just what he displayed on the surface. The essential Bill — as revealed most in his poetry — was a man of insightful depth, spiritual seeking, and profound compassion.

CONTENTS

Distances: Selected Poems

GERMAN

Every woman adores a fascist.
—Sylvia Plath

Order, I cried clicking my,
swishing my swagger stick, marching around the room.
Oh but the room wouldn't listen,
nothing would brace itself, the walls
wouldn't snap to. Pictures askew,
dishes dirty, carpet sown with crumbs and fingernails,
records scattered and jacketless, fuzzy with dust —
Oh dull! Oh heavy
sleepless torpor of amputees from the western front!
Grandfather's clock, old movies, newspapers,
Dresden china. Jews
mooing in boxcars. ORDER ORDER ORDER, I cried,
but the room soiled itself like a frightened soldier, ach!
So I kick it in,
shattering dishes, windows, skulls
of pedestrian friends with my shiny boot, break through
like a hairy giant
to Asgard, vistas, clouds, the distant Sturm und Drang —
Freude, schoener Goetterfunken,
Tochter aus Elysium!

A FAREWELL TO SURREALISM

*There is often a passage in even the most thoroughly interpreted
dream which has to be left obscure . . . This is the dream's navel, the
spot where it reaches down into the unknown.*

— Freud

1.

I have come to the place of knots,
like a donkey. Knots that coil and stretch,
dip into heat and hold, like lungs,
enormous roots, whistling lianas,
wires and veins, all the ineffable
rags of the poor. Knots like eyeballs,
sistrums, tits and umbrellas. Slowly,
the lines stretch out like waves on a far
horizon. Sand. Blood. Rocks
of course stand around like a pen.
They laugh at my underpants.

2.

I go through the window,
gently, nothing is shattered,
fall against the porch post,
something is buzzing, furniture
is black. I'm twisting
my face to wake up, trip over
the coffee table and float
facedown to the floor.

3.

Dreams are weird. God, who gives them,
gentle as sharks, fierce as bluegills,
says: I am. I lie around
with my antenna up, watching
the flickering screen. What does it mean?
I read the footnotes. Freud and Jung
give each other the finger. Bly
sits in his wig and hose, like Johnson.
I sniff my weirdness like a dog.
    "TRANSLUCENT ANGEL — FIRE INSIDE!"
    I tell my friends. "A GHOST
    LIKE THE MILKY WAY AROUND MY HEAD,
    AND NOISE LIKE BOMBERS!"
                              They love me.
Smile and bring me wine. I pass out
on their couch. My head is a stone.
Bladder fills by itself. Heart grows mossy.
Mouth is sealed with mortar.
        Still,
at some ungodly hour,
two little girls
jump on me;
I rise
through the weeds
and hug them.

THE NAME OF MY TERROR

If I could name it, I think,
Practically dead, I would be cured.
It *must* have a name,
Simple, like fish, girl, bird.

It is dumb, I know this,
Or rather it doesn't prefer
Talking about itself, it just occurs
Like bird, girl, fish.

Sometimes I almost see it, moving
Around me, sort of a swirl
Of bubbles, sepia ink
In the water, spreading.

It will let me sleep, yes;
Indeed it has spread so thin
I think I could lie in it forever,
Having no need of the word.

I think if I called it by name
My eyes would fly from my head,
My nose would fill with stones, my ears
Would bleed, my tongue creak like a bed,

And everyone come running, running
To see me get my wish:
The name for the thing as simple
As girl, bird, fish.

PORCINE DAYS

Remember the hog days in Biscoe,
    And the Durocs a-chuggin' their mash?
Oh I wouldn't trade it for Frisco,
    And I'd hand over all of my trash

Just to be on a johnboat at twilight,
    Where the river turns into a bog,
And to see through the water by my light
    A catfish big as a hog,

To be covered with doughbait and crawlers,
    To sit as you never have sat,
In a pith helmet big as a trawler,
    A-dreamin' of cornmeal and fat;

Or out on a farmpond at daybreak,
    Thick with lilies and frogs,
A-hearin' the hounds in the canebrake,
    And the lonesome oink of the hogs.

Oh that wonderful land o' my dreamin'!
    I can smell it as good as my clothes —
Where the bogs and ricefields are steamin',
    Where the Cache River just barely flows,

Where Corly Combs often shot him
    A hunderd rabbits to bits,
Where "Lunker Bass" Holly caught him
    His all-time champeen fish,

And took it all over the county,
  And to every human and dog,
Showed it like God's great bounty
  And said: "Say, lookit this hog."

Oh to go everwhere in your Sweet-Orr
  Overalls snapped at the bib;
Oh to bring to the boys at the feedstore
  A truckful of barbecue rib,

Or to be at the Crown Fillin' Station
  A-talkin' 'bout hippies and bass,
A-sippin' our Nehi and waitin'
  For a stranger to stop in for gas.

Oh to have some Red Man tobacco
  To spit on the hogs where they lay,
To lean on a fence or a tractor,
  Sayin': "Hot enough fer yuh today?"

With dirt underneath of your eyelids,
  Your hands all gritty and dry,
And the sizzlin' of zillions of flylets
  As the buzzards hang in the sky.

And while Wilda Ilene's feelin' poorly,
  I'd be pickin' at woodticks and fleas,
A-rockin' with Lloyd in the dooryard,
  Covered with stubble and grease,

With hog jowls and trotters to chew on,
  With shotguns laid on our laps,
To shoot most anythin' movin'
  And throw the coonhounds the scraps.

CUT MYSELF SHAVING
WHILE THINKING UP A POEM

The stars are rooted in you, I thought,
nourished by your dreaming, tiny dying
flowers that measure distance. They are the
secret you have planted, and they flash
over the light years, anchored in the
rich soil of your wishing. I think of Einstein
traveling in a train, looking out
the window at time and space:
what did he long for, what had he lost?
O lost in the black well what we are bound to —
SONAFABITCH, I yelled,
spotting myself again, alone in the mirror, thinking:
I am going. I am going away.

SMOKE

Every morning, smoke in the air,
something on fire somewhere,
the faultless houses still asleep,
oblong patches of light
on the clapboard, green and white and grey,
the trees behind them pale and stiff as straw.
Smoke in the air,
a woodpecker knocks,
a mourning dove is cooing,
I am going
crazy, where is the smoke
coming from, from God?
Pigeons whirl up from the pavement,
the vacant lot is loaded with junk,
its gullies frozen solid.
Smoke, smoke,
and I am going
crazy. Early morning.

STONED

After we buried Jamie
we all got stoned
Simmons had the grass
we hovered
hysterically in the kitchen
making joints
it looked almost
like a sewing bee.
We watched the first one
start, the grave
pentecostal flame
going from hand to hand.
I took it —
Oh it burned my eyes
with joy, that smell
like freshcut sandalwood!
I could have cried
but giggled insead.
All night long
I wandered, giggling,
around that house, Duke's apartment!
I went from room
to room, how barren
to be a bachelor,
empty, empty!
I thought
of Jamie's widow,
whose hand I'd held in church,
tight as talons.
And now

right now
Jamie's piecing frowning eyes
his bristling crewcut
rise up
before me, Jamie's ghost
pissed off!
"Oh bullshit, Zander,
bullshit!" But where were you
that night,
how could you leave
such good company?
Dear terrified
intense and angry
friend, you are
my Charon, who drove your car
on purpose off
the bridge (that night
I didn't know it, only knew
you were dead,
patient at last
with politics —
your lonely letter
integrated
a branch of the Murfreesboro,
Tennessee, P.O., but we
are your people, Jamie,
as you know.) Later
I found a guitar
and played some blues, Jamie
would have like this,
I mused, and tried to impress

a girl, who seemed
friendly enough, I mean
she giggled too. I mean
this is what you do,
you put a man in the ground
and see him off
with dignity and tears, but love
(as someone said)
calls us to the things
of this world.
I'd call it grief,
the terrible hysteria
that kept me giggling.
At least I know
I was stoned and drunk
and sick as hell
in the morning, gagging
long black strands of vomit
out in the cornfield
with the crows at dawn.

DYING OF LOVE

In the Renaissance, men were dying of love:
You learn that in school. Held on a gloved fist,
The falcon was a simile for my lord,
And a fortress meant that first, difficult kiss.

She was a world of ideas and aspirations,
In a long gown with jewels on it;
Neatly, she swung her farthingale to go,
And the sight of her foot produced a sonnet.

The flow of her gown seemed like the fields of Aragon,
A ruff and partlet hid her snow-white breasts;
Seen at a distance, she suggested journeys,
And my lord only waited on her behest

Ere he moved his forces into the light,
Flying her flag, his orders sharp and pure.
But she was a cruel commander, and rarely opened
Her cherry lips, to tell him how he might serve her.

So instead of riding into the field
At her command, he would brood at night,
Look at the moon, compare it to his lady,
Walk through his empty rooms, and then sit down to write,

But another lord was hit with the same dart,
And though it charged his blood he never contracted
The same disease, and instead of waiting
Upon the lady for her command, he acted,

And laid siege with all his might, and what
Had appeared to be a fortress hadn't been.
There was a heart, lonely like yours and mine,
And various bruises on her snowwhite skin.

And this lord, too, died of love,
But it was in bed, upon a pool of sweat,
And if, later, he found the time for verse,
As a peacock shows its tail, he showed his wit.

In the Renaissnce, men were dying of love:
You learn it in school. There were those who died
Amused at woman's inconstancy, how she was human,
And those who weren't, and were never satisfied.

THE COMING OF GREEN

is subtle, the coming of little points,
little embroideries, against the grey and bristling
armies of the hills; the buds unfurl,
tiny and cautious, yellow as much as green;
leaves poke out of the soil, or whorl
like green and newly discovered shells,
spears and tongues and little green hearts,
the veins clear and important — now
the infinite complexities begin:
blue grass, bent grass, oat grass, crab grass,
white oak, black oak, red oak, still
the green spreads with a sigh,
green like a water color, plain as day;
and flowers, bright and explosive;
the petals fall, the green creeps up,
hiding the fruit, the nests of birds and squirrels,
it closes in as it opens, wider and wider,
heavy, solid, massive,
pounds of green, like dough, rising,
the hills groan with the weight of green,
heat presses down, green, green,
green with its cheeks puffed out, holding its breath,
the houses smothered in green, green
through the buzzing screen, the sky a hole in the green,
green, green, in the depths of which,
should you lose yourself in the darkest spot,
the center of all that green,
you would be where you always wanted to go,
you would surrender like the hills
to green, and its torpid, solid weight
would sink you in ultimate green,
the ostrich fern, the moss on a log

where an ant is stalking, there in the shade
you would fizz like a swamp where cattails nod,
and lilies lie flat and undisturbed
on the clotted, mossy water.

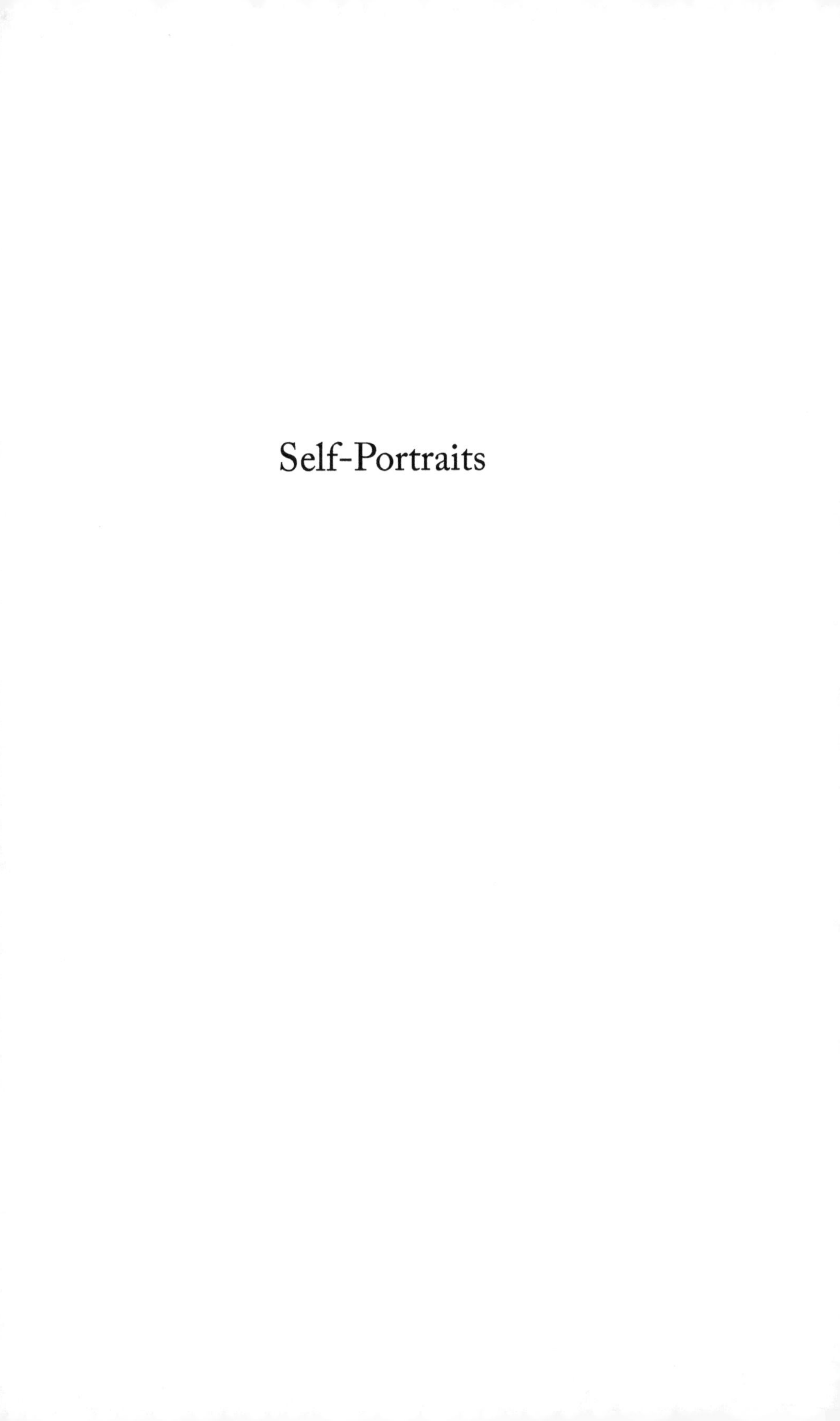

Self-Portraits

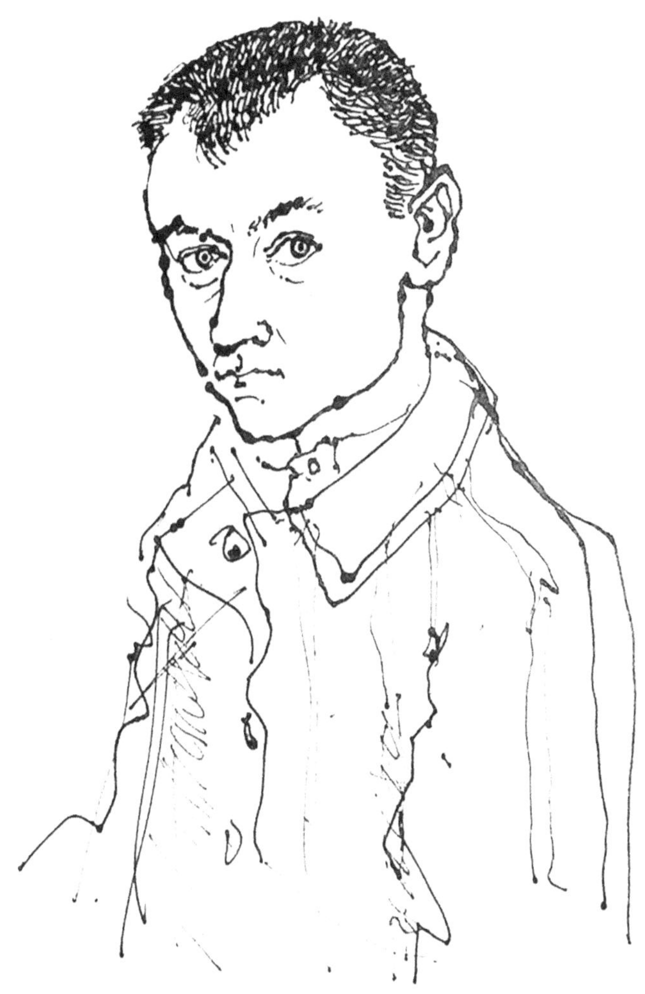

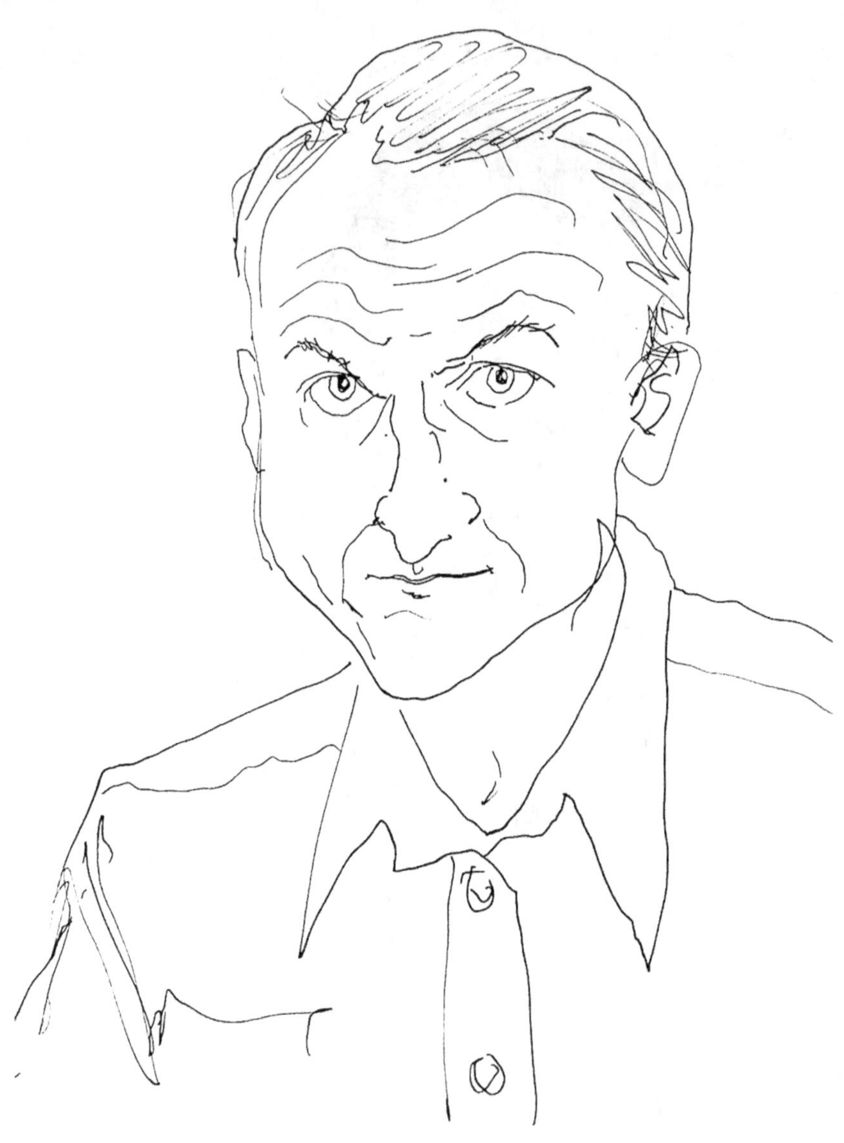

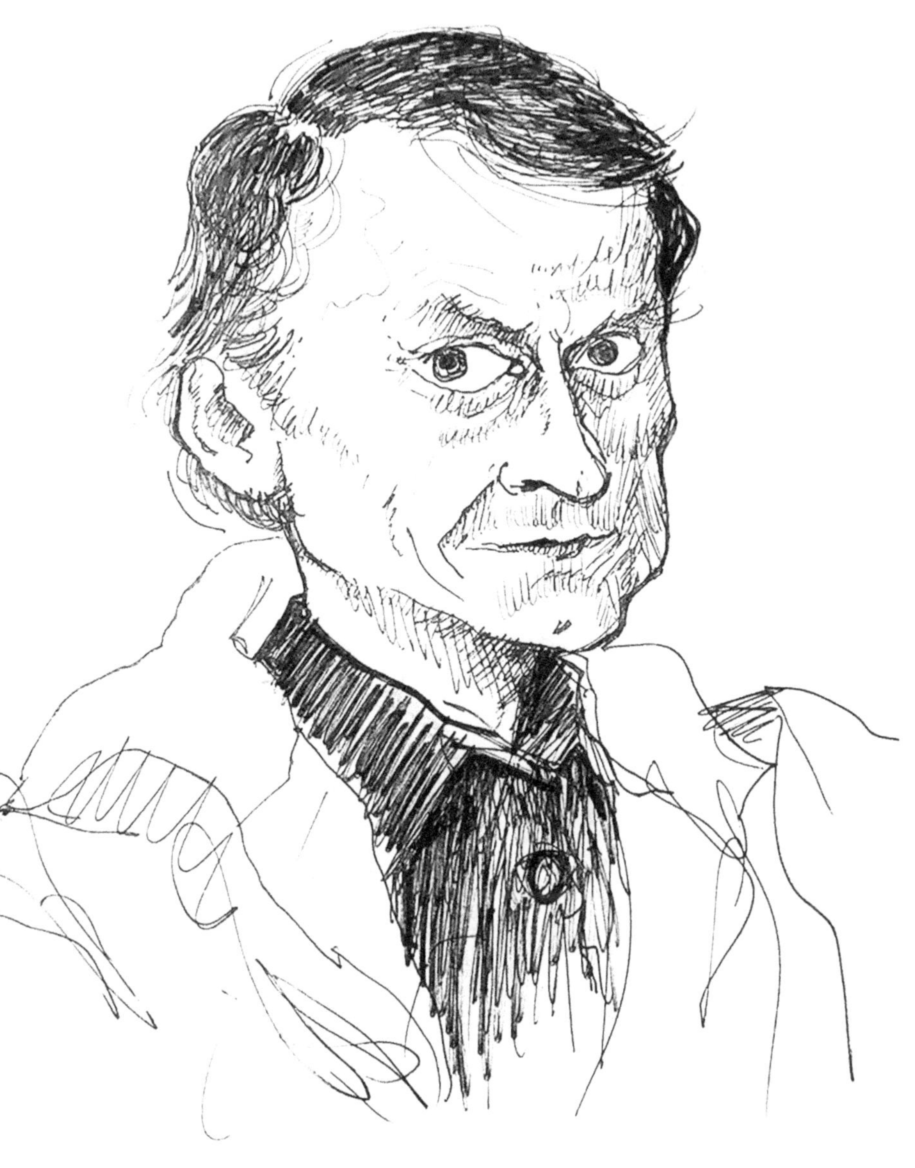

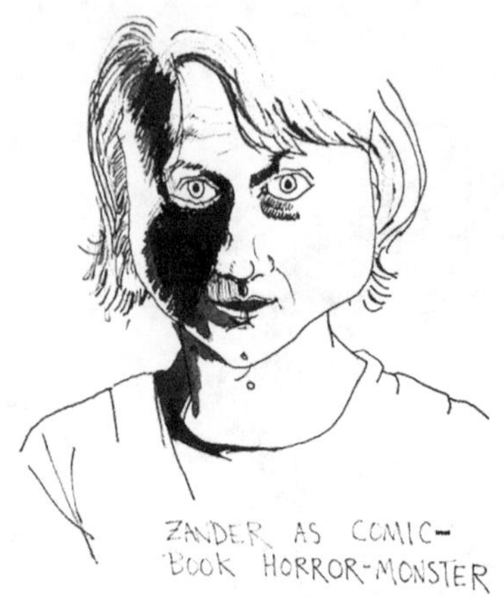

ZANDER AS COMIC-
BOOK HORROR-MONSTER

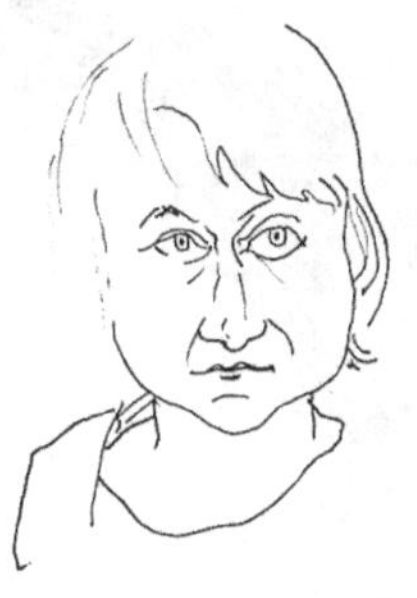

ZANDER AS A
CORRUPT
ROMAN SENATOR

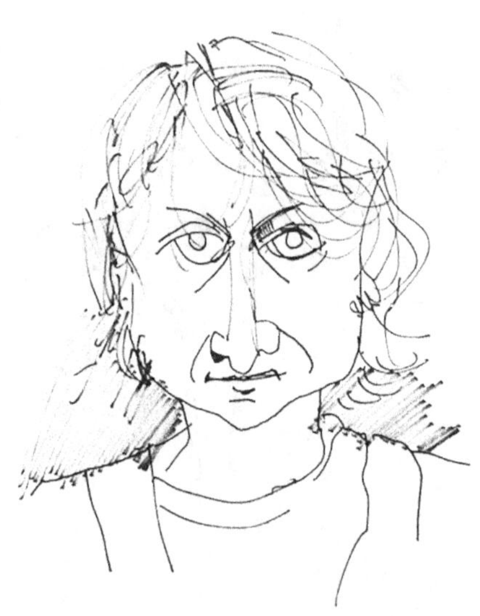

ZANDER AS SENSITIVE POET

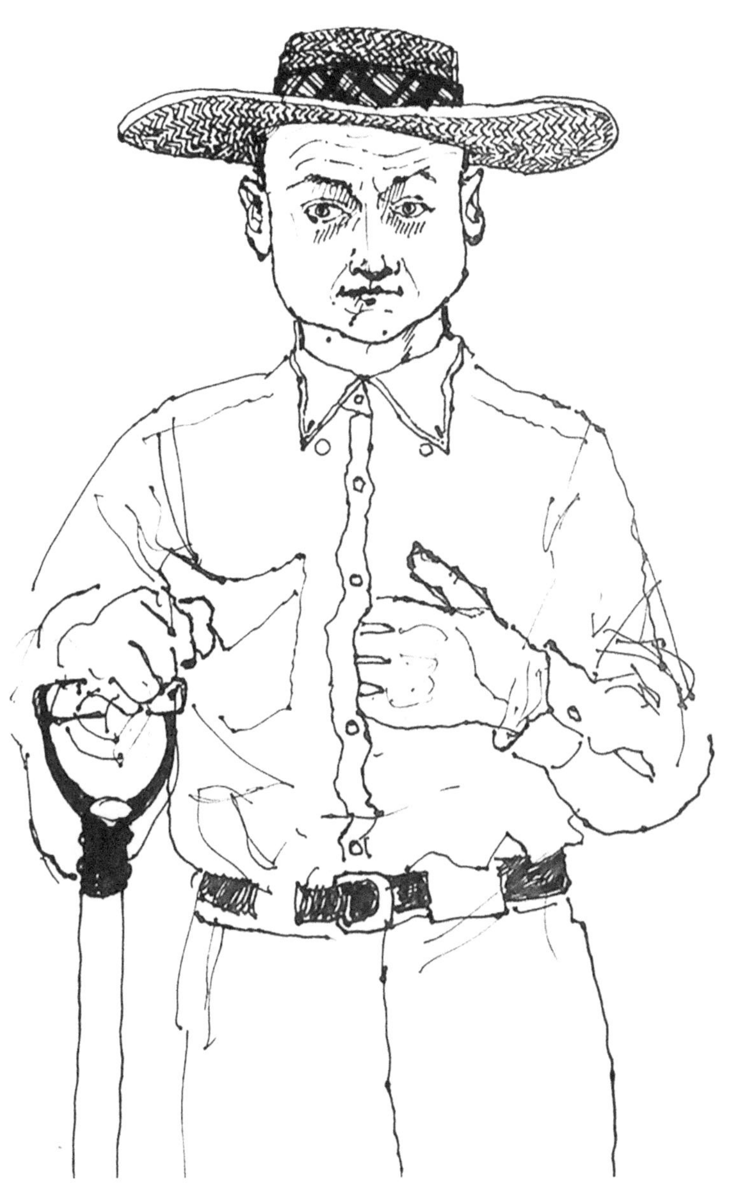

Winter Trees: Selected Poems

TRUTH

What is truth? asked Pilate, philosophically,
and thus was doomed never to know it.
Judicious, patient, never overbearing,
he could weigh the issues, he could discuss them
in a mild voice. I guess he'd raise it sometimes,
after too much wine, with friends —
but we have access only to his public self,
trying to do what's right, even
(let's be fair) what's democratic.
And he tries a compromise
(the scourging — that was his idea).
But the people make their choice. He thinks:
"I cannot stop it. I can feel the waves
even up here. Something
is happening. There is this man,
scourged, bleeding, mocked.
What can I do? There are so many,
so many truths, so many courses.
Sometimes I think a man is foolish
to believe in anything.
Let it go. This man is not to blame.
I find no fault in this just man.
Nor in me, nor in anyone!"
He washes his hands. He is like us.
He is only human. He cannot know what truth is.
Sometimes it rises up from the dead,
in dreams, an angry outburst,
a razor at the throat. There is no comfort then
in being only human.

SILENCE

— For Frank Pein, and myself

Even the greatest silent movies needed
something more than Keaton, Lloyd, or Chaplin —
someone, usually not at all a genius,
thumping the keys, slower or faster
as the scene demanded. Even now,
when one might wish for silence
(fed up with modern noise), imagine
seeing those films in perfect silence —
bound and gagged, not even having the solace
of your own laughter in the dark
and soundproof room. Silence!
and another world unfolds, as chilling
as a city siren, hovering, ominous
as an eagle with a snake,
the unshared images of dreams,
the allegory of the cave
but without meaning — watching, watching
with bitter longing and elation,
knowing at last that Truth is distance —
as if this light were all in all,
this black and white, these glowing
pratfalls, wringings of hands,
the chase — they seem the efforts
of fools at best, of empty forms at worst,
and only you can see it, only you
are like the universe, with nothing else
to turn to. And now it floats there, hours, days,
like sunlight on the arctic snow.
Listen! Not even a birdsong.
This could be Nothing, but you feel it.

MAMMALS

And God said: Let there be mammals, maybe.
And there appeared like dustballs in the shadows
shrews and voles and hedgehogs, or whatever,
sniffing tentatively. All were tiny;
some had whiskers; some had ears
as big as their heads. All were warm and furry,
drawn to each other's warmth, touching.
Some had bushy tails and crouched
on the highest limbs, picking insects
off each other. And the mammals held,
hugged and humped and squeezed their young out —
clamor, clamor! — who fixed themselves
on the source. And flowers opened
on dogwood and laurel, planetetherium glided
from limb to limb, marsupials waddled
with bags of babies. And there appeared
burrowing spots, nests and dens, a need
for tomorrow, a lively network of knowing.
And the mammals left the trees and shadows,
staying close, gophers, rabbits, moles
looking for holes, snarling things
with sharp-cusped teeth, lemurs looking
in three dimensions. And the waters rose,
volcanoes spouted, the air grew cool
and grasses spread. And the mammals hunkered together,
hunted together, shook with fever and chills,
grew fat and old: lumbering, horny brontops;
herds of horses; tapirs; rhinos;
long-necked camels munching on treetops;
otters slapping at fish; the great sloth
rising on its hind legs;
mastodons with swaying trunks, marching

over the land bridge. And as the chill breath
of the ice descended, things kept moving;
pines came down from the mountains, wolves in packs,
the solitary sabertooth,
bison, musk ox, babies prodded
and waited for. Some of the more
precocious and prehensile had a feeling
that was beyond them, made them nervous,
made them carve and scrape and seek out pigments,
made them dream. And now the mammal
looked to the stars, noting its nakedness,
its germs. It tried to fix itself.
The snow blew in its eyes. The body muttered,
grew erect like any predator.
It carved some more. The air grew warm;
the mammal found itself alone
in the wilderness. It would make kings.
Make death go blank. Make sprezzatura
and pundonor and Lebensraum.
And God said: Let there be space.

AUTUMN

In the woods I found
the carcass of a crow,
almost hidden
by leaves and glacial rubble,
its wings spread out on the ground
like an insignia.
How long had it been there?
Long enough,
so breathing through my mouth,
I knelt and plucked
some feathers from a wing
to tie a small
black caddis fly
that hatches in the spring.
Oh what a lesson!
crow's wing,
caddis fly, a trout
going up my bloodstream.
I plucked those feathers,
hardly daring to breathe.

TWO SONNETS FOR ALEX

1.
Teeth, cheekbones, eye sockets, the hard terrain
Of my own skull, kissed for me in bed —
But then you stopped, seemed surprised, and said:
"I smell carnations!" Your nose touching a vein
That jutted from my temple, as if my brain
Were squeezed too tight. Carnations in my head!
You must have made them bloom, the watershed
In that vast land I wanted to explain:
A desert shimmering away in light,
Where I'd imagined everything. But you!
You were no goddess, recognized on sight
From dreams of death, from the poetry I wrote;
Discoverer, you told me flowers grew
In ground I thought was lunar and remote.

2.
If I say I'm jealous, don't think I'm a cramped,
Squint-eyed redneck full of mean suspicions,
Or that I want your love's abundance stamped
"Classified data" for my secret missions.
My gut aches sometimes, that's all. It can't be cured.
I know no therapy to make the mating
Any more sensible, any less weird
With pangs, pressures, preening, and parading.
I love you as a gander loves a goose —
No human love is more enduring! Inviting
His lady to be had, he cannot choose
But strike the same pose as he does for fighting.
Call it a pose. Still, my love's not light.
If even I so treat it, I will fight.

HAMLET CONTEMPLATE THE SKULL
OF GABRIEL EDMUND, RECENTLY BORN

Calcium, carbon, clay that the potter left
Open for filling — oh what a piece of work
Is . . . drool? Strange how even my words have grown
Uncertain, the graveyard humor struck dumb
By this little skull I hold, my hand smelling
Of antiseptic soap . . . alas, poor baby!
If I let go, something would snap; it can't
Support what it's doing here; it needs me now
More than my father's ghost. Oh hand, oh head!
This poetry insists, will not hold still,
Will not be meaningless. I bring the face
Up close to mine and look into the wide
Blue eyes — or are they blue? The brow is furrowed.
I worry about those pimply, hectic cheeks,
Blue veins instead of hair on top, the heartbeat
Pulsating in the seam, the four corners,
The skull hole — I don't dare touch it! There are things
In there undreamt of in your philosophy. . .
I mean, the cerebrum forming out of ooze,
An expanding universe of splitting cells.
Slowly, sound starts working up inside,
Ka-ka-ka-ka, like a cough or catching of breath,
Bursts forth, surprises him — the startle reflex,
Hands shoot up in the air — flailing hands,
Expressive hands, fingers (not mere fists)
Moving, conducting the Philharmonic, yes!
He is believable. I will not let him
Fall. Whatever I was, I've made it better.
Screaming! Oh little skull. Fill up with teeth.

SEEING MY SON

Splitting wood on the snowy slope that drops
behind my house, I take a breather from
a knotty slab of hickory and look out
over the frozen lake. Goalie, I call,
the wind taking my voice and raising spindrifts.
Goalie! Again, louder. Dropping the maul
and starting down to get beyond the trees,
I suddenly see him, a dot on the disc of snow,
the blankness stretching from the bristling
side of the mountain — little lake,
but like the tundra now. Black-hooded Goalie,
little moonface, fat and padded, the dog
bounding before him like a loose basketball,
almost out of bounds — both so small,
I think they must disappear. Four years old,
so bleak, so brave, so far away
and in focus, absolutely silent, falling —
lying still just once, too long — up again,
circling back, the dog making larger circles
around him. All that space for running! It makes
the emptiness look fun. I should call him back,
but then? I have work to do before the storm.
        Later, beside the stove, the dog stretched out
at our feet, the house so full of noise and warmth
that an icy peace will seem to grow, elsewhere,
I will read to him and his little brother —
eyebrows, eyelids, close as a Holbein portrait —
"This Is the House That Jack Built," which they know
by heart. I don't see into that. I don't
see anything but snow. Goalie. Goalie.

HOLDING

I have held dead things in my hands.
None was human. Summer, swimming with
my children; their sleek, living bodies
are all over me. We duck each other, bob
to the surface, breathing. Winter, ice
spreads on the lake, its veins go deep, its surface
sets like a face in grief. It fills with snow.
The children, bundled up, come running with
a dead horned owl they've found in the woods,
rare to the touch, rigid, clear,
its eyes squeezed shut. I take it from them by the legs,
its feet with their talons doubled like
an old man's fists. I hold it upside-
down like poultry, watch the bundle of feathers fall
open — brown, tan, russet,
umber, burnt sienna, fluff, the white at the throat.
The wings are stiff, so with my other hand I stretch
one out, startled by its length,
its soft flight feathers wet, disheveled,
the barbs askew. The children lose interest.
What does it mean, this innocence, this leverage?
Will death ever instruct me? The human, holding forth!
Cupboards, windows, shelves, unnecessary
dreamwork. I toss the carcass in the woods.
If it were human, I would hold
that mystery, a body to bury.

WINTER TREES

Dissected trees, nerves and veins
Laid bare against the antiseptic blue —
What are they but the green brain
Of summer, open to my view?

An opening for *ubi sunt*!
The poet reflecting on a warmer past,
The childhood with its scummy pond,
The dirty book that couldn't last.

Where is the prickly *weight* of green,
Its hoots and croakings that filled up the night,
June bugs pinging against the screen,
My rage at tiny things that bite?

What clotted leaves! What oaks and maples!
What looping vines where Tarzan might have swung!
What fierce buzzing in this brain
All summer long! What thoughts that stung!

Where is the solid stuff I wanted?
Where is the tissue that's been scraped away?
Where is the hustle of the ant,
The grasshopper drunk in the hay?

The Mind of God! Now, while it sleeps,
Is the time to look into its mysteries.
See how stark it is, yet deep.
How empty. Save for winter trees.

Drawings of Family,
Friends, Children,
Dogs, Musicians

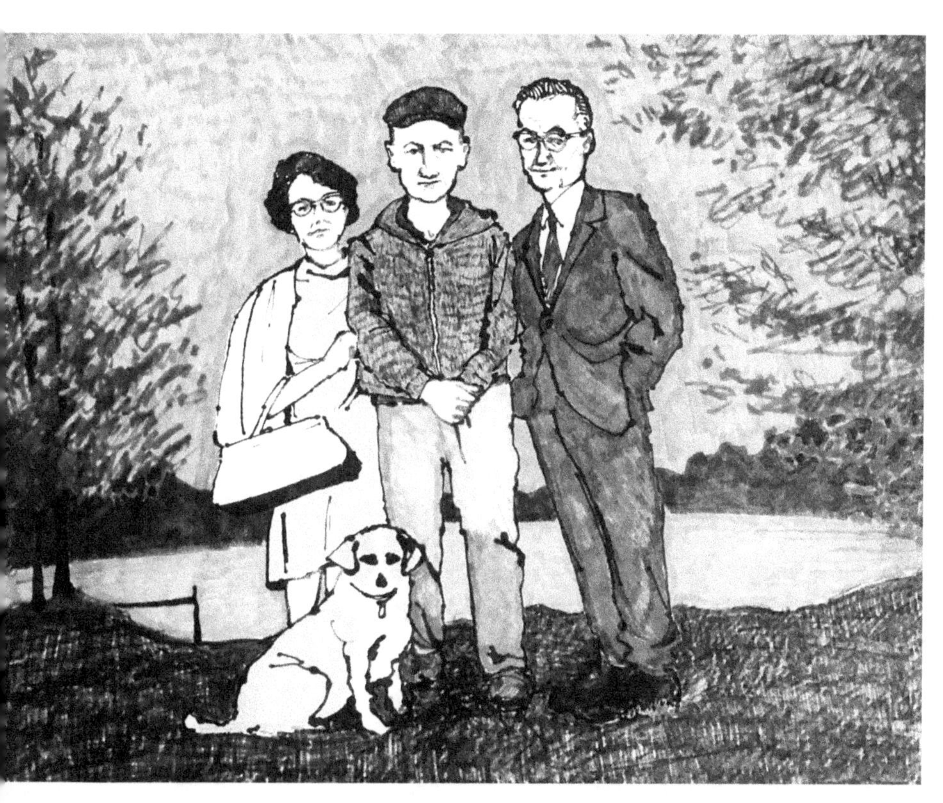

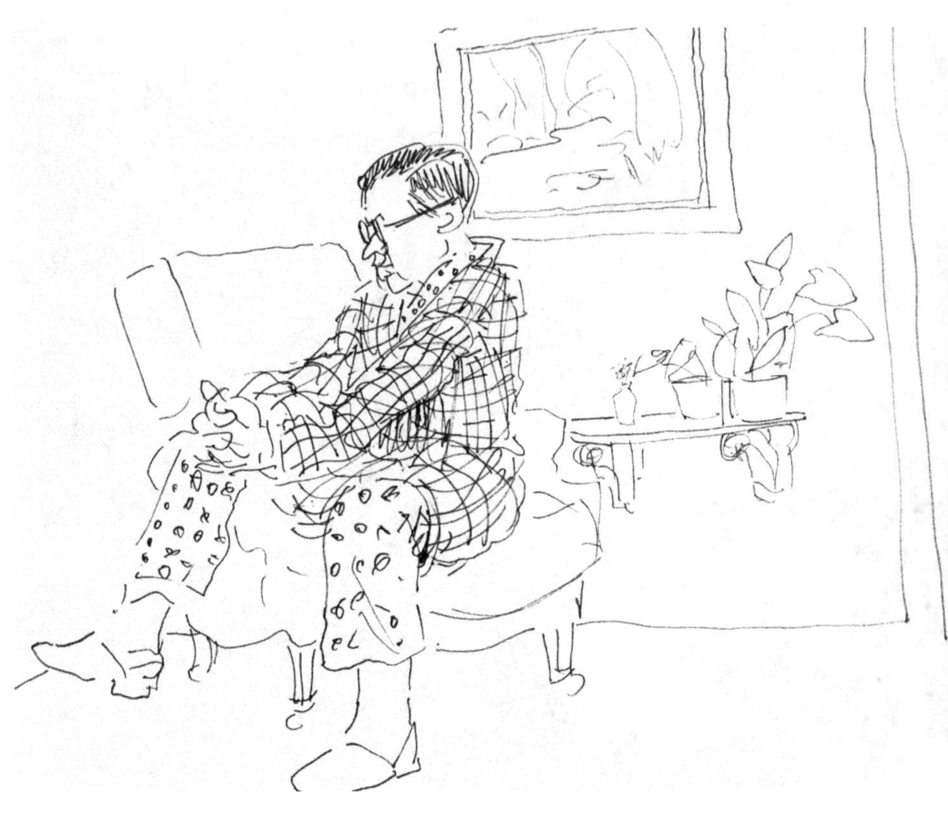

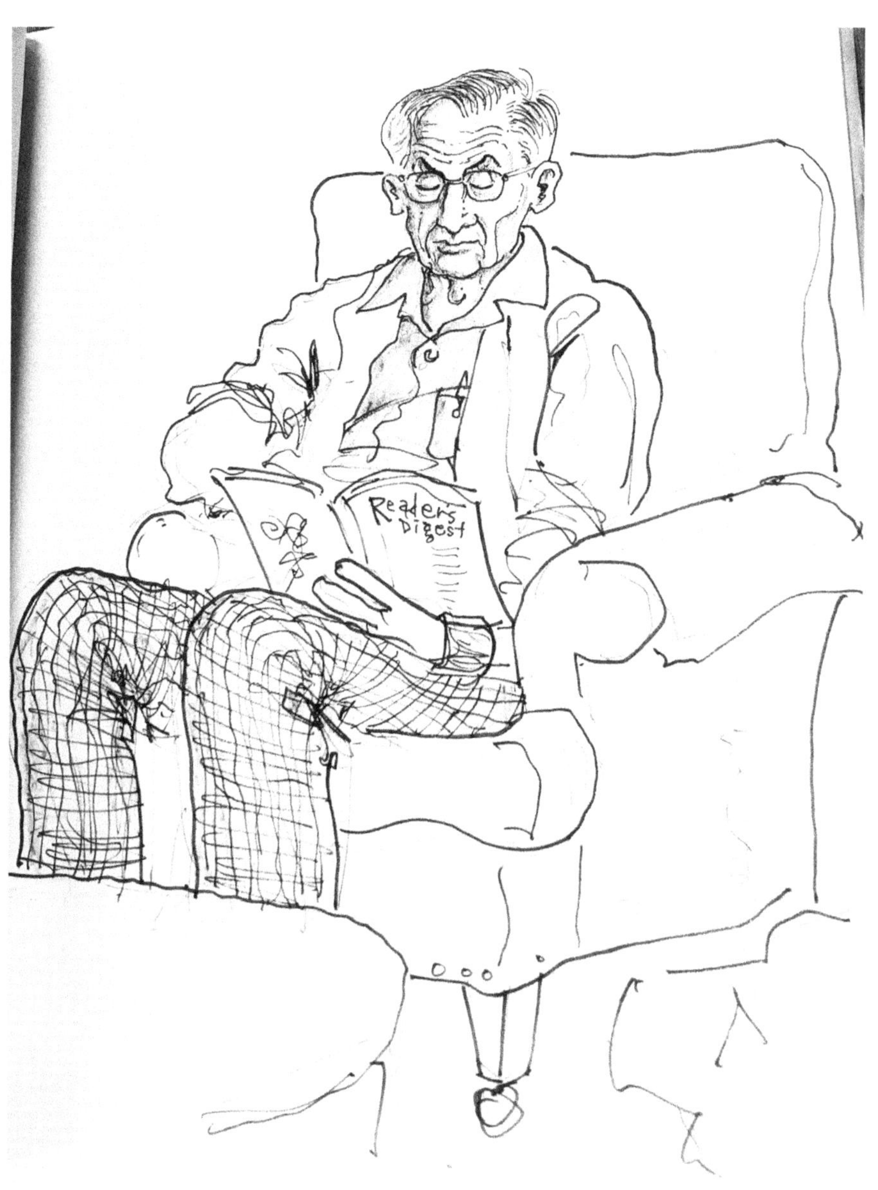

Reader's Digest

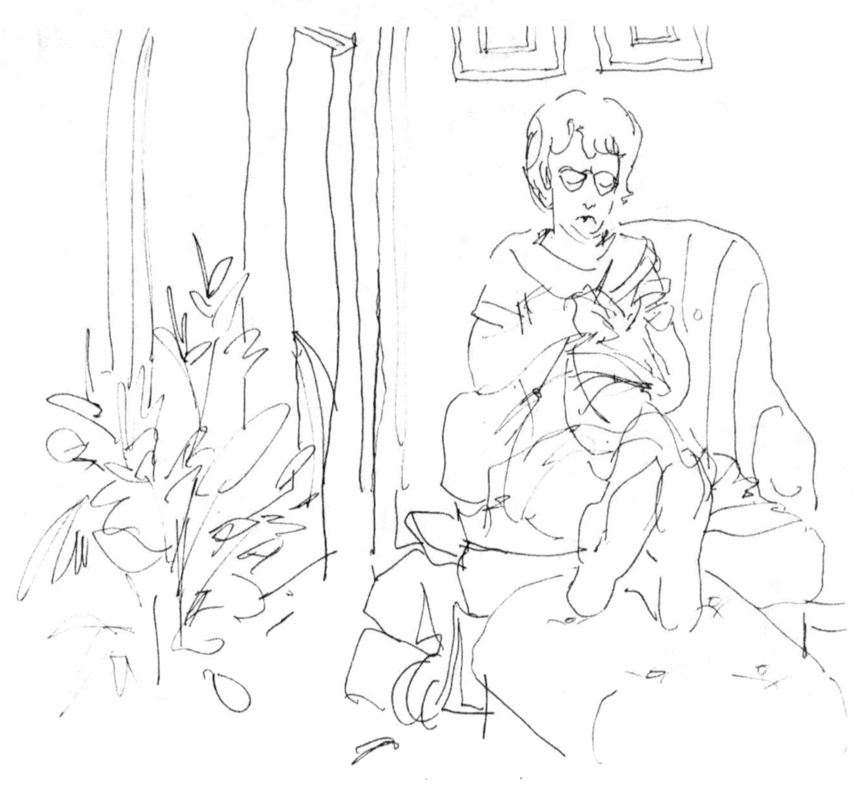

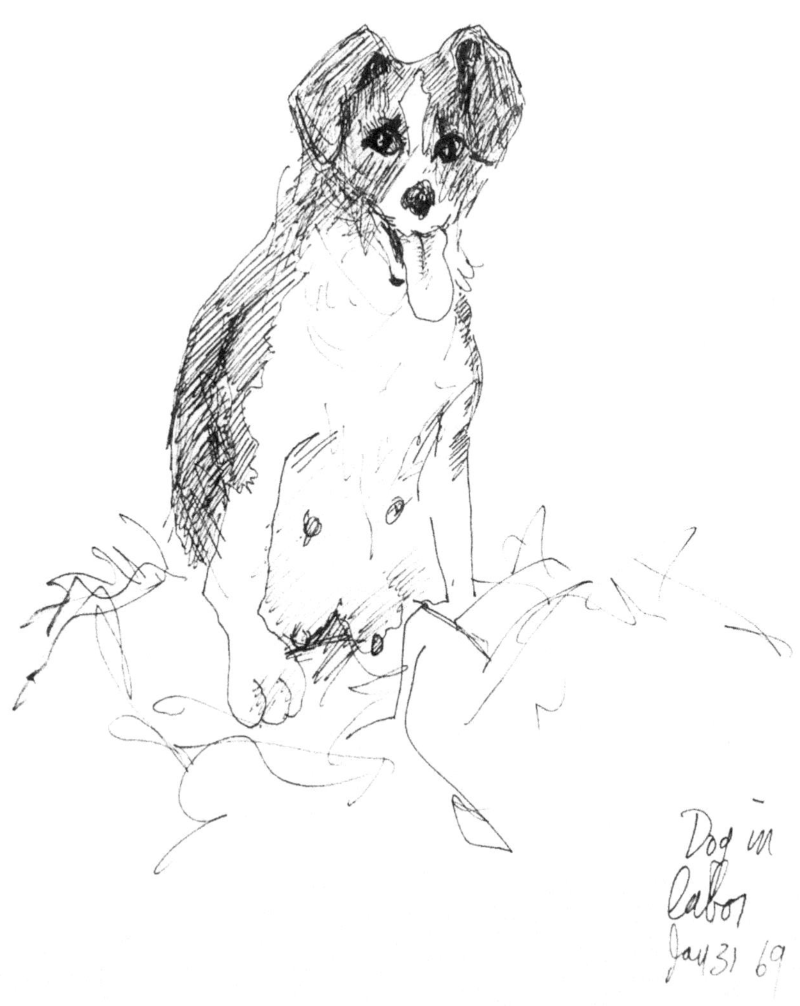

Dog in
Labor
Jan 31 69

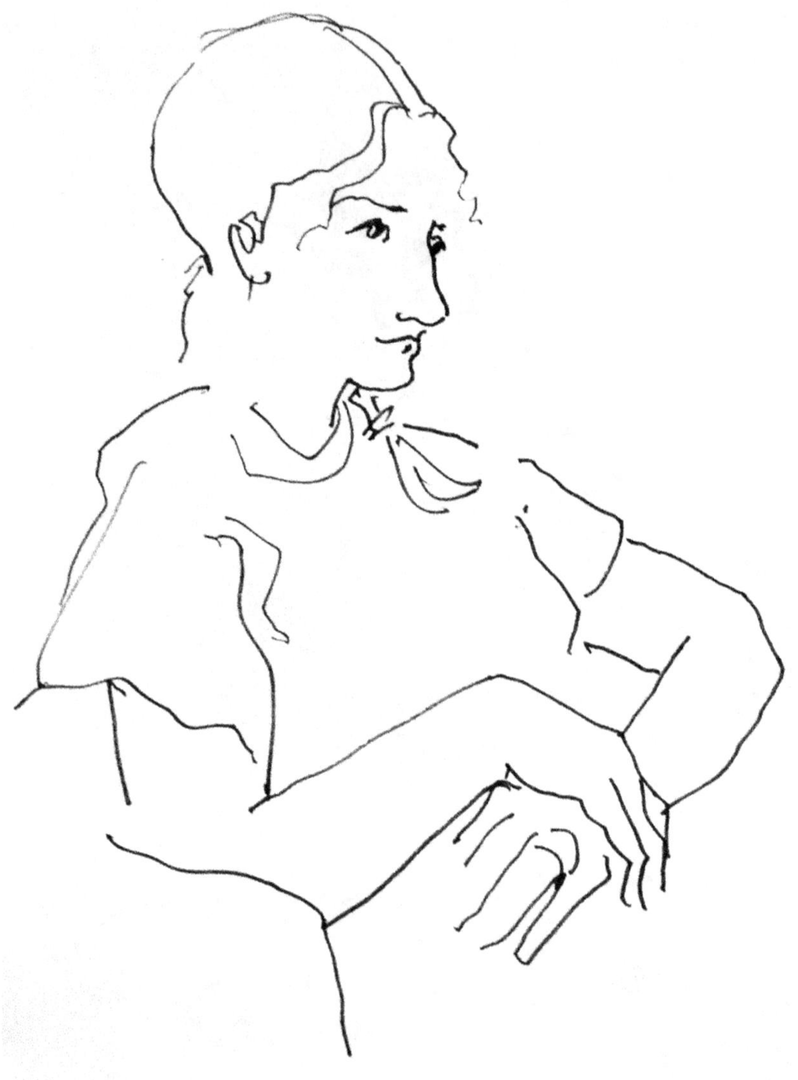

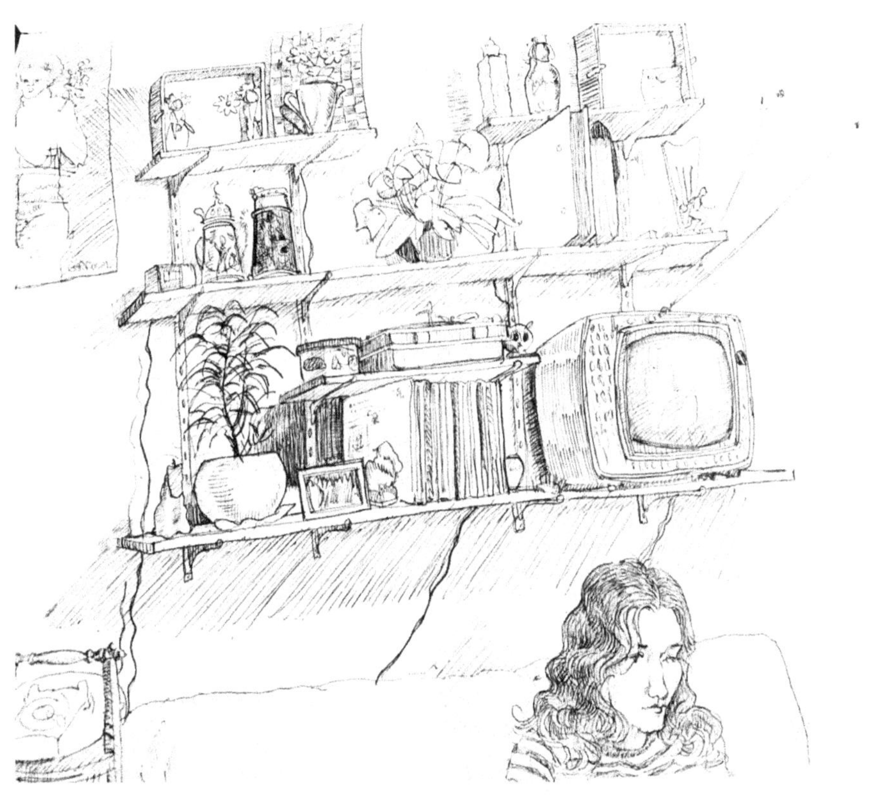

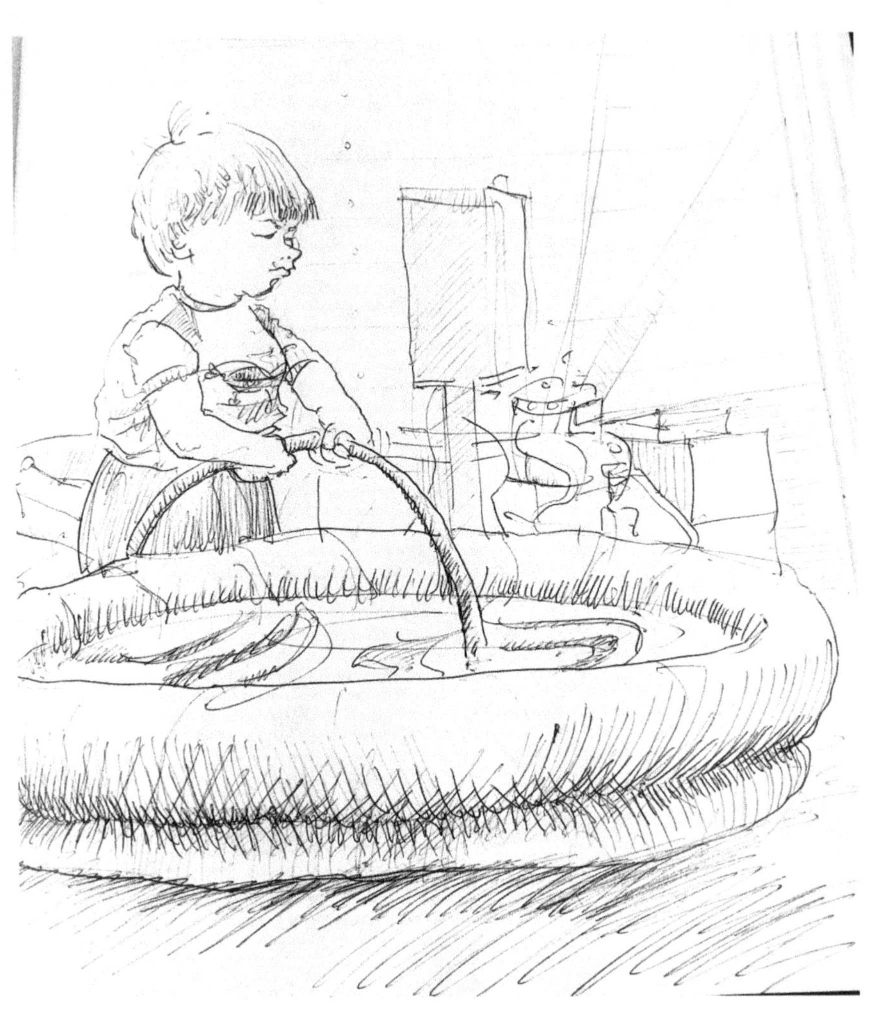

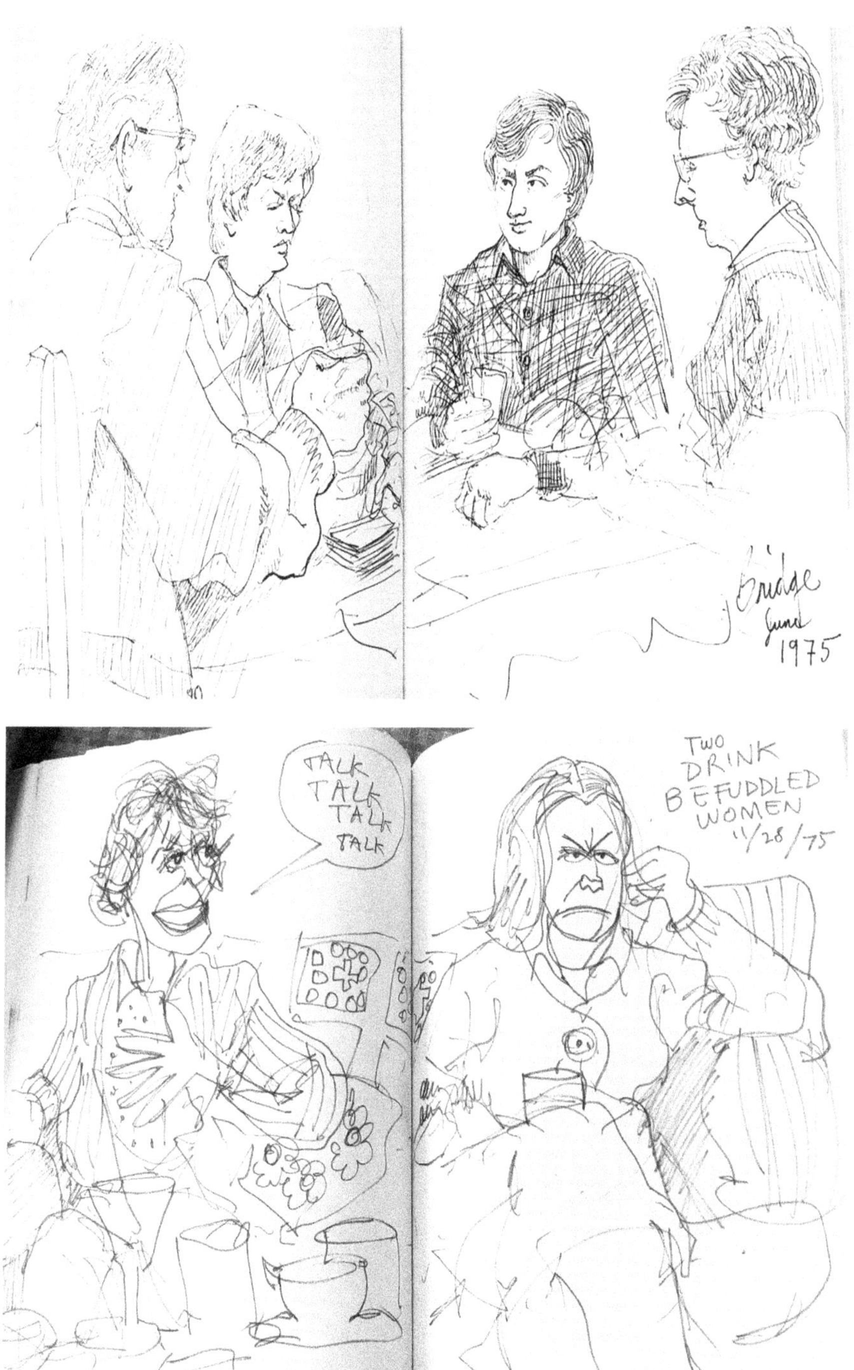
Bridge
June
1975
TALK
TALK
TALK
TALK
TWO
DRINK
BEFUDDLED
WOMEN
11/28/75

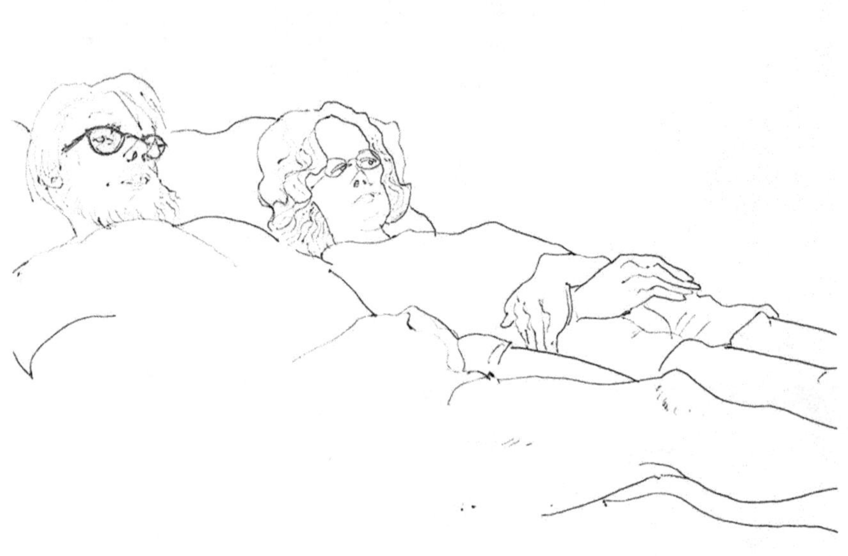

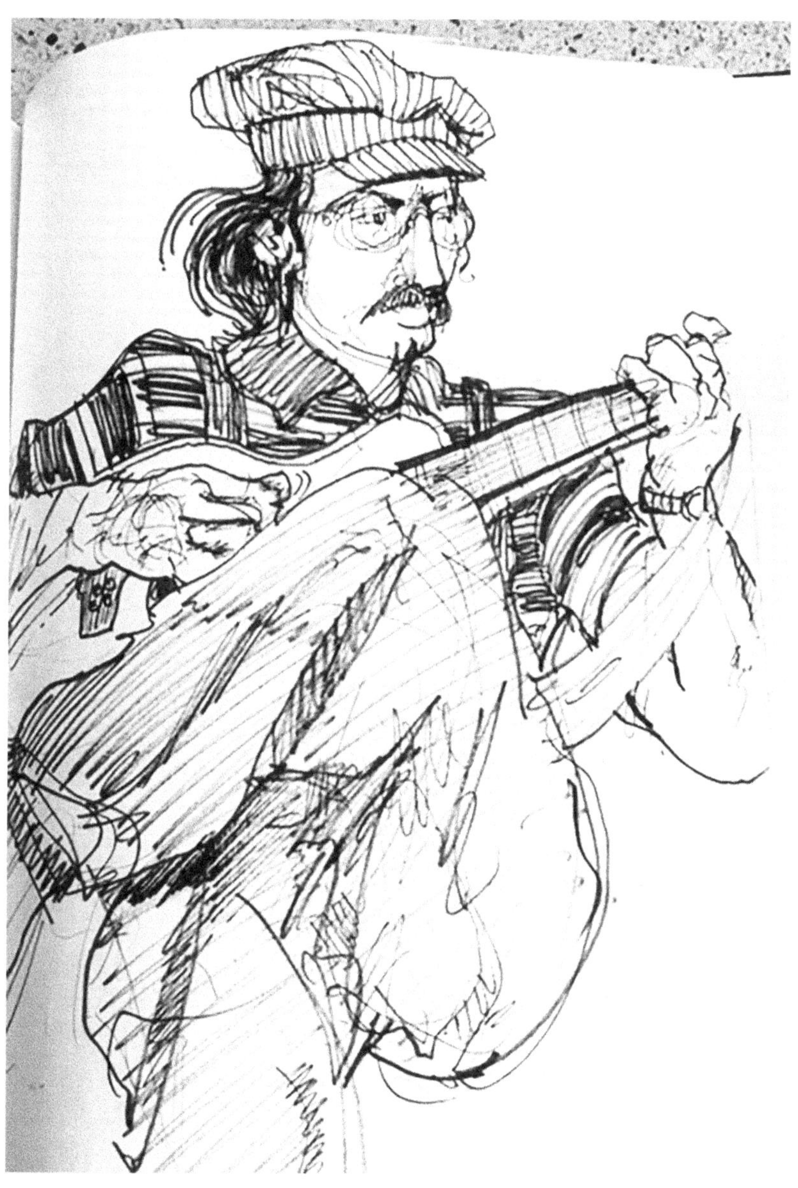

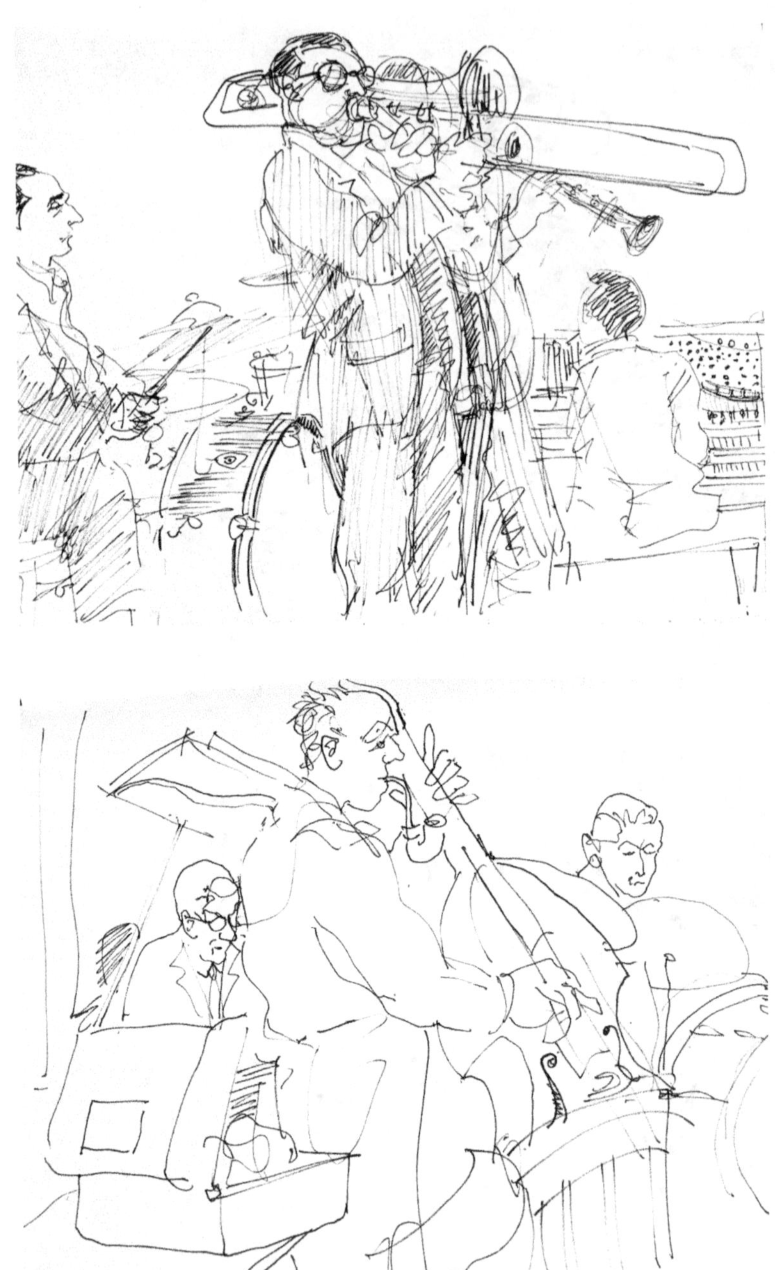

Gone Haywire and Other Old Sayings:
Selected Poems

AUTHOR'S NOTE

All these poems come from a suite-in-progress I call *Old Sayings*. They are based on English clichés, bromides, idiomatic locutions, &c. Actually, "based on" is not correct; sometimes, a phrase is the starting point for a poem (e.g. "What Do You Want for Nothing?"), but, at other times, a poem begins from the usual dark source and the title comes later.

The point is, this is a suite, not a sequence (like a sonnet sequence), so I feel free to use whatever starting point works, as well as whatever form or content works. So far, I've written everything from a prose poem to rime royal, from comic verse to rather heavy stuff, from poems with personal content to those with the impersonal emotion Eliot called for, lean poems and fat poems, bellowing poems and sotto voce poems.

The many phrases I've found, it seems to me, still have life, if heard from a certain angle; they represent the living language as it is now, powered by living breath. As titles, they seem to give a shape, a sort of verbal keystone, to all sorts of wacky and profound moods.

There are, I think, two meanings to the rubric *Old Sayings*. There is the one I originally intended (clichés &c.), and there is the fact that these poems are clearly in the voice of an increasingly old guy saying stuff.

— William Zander

HYMN: PLAIN AS DAY

Dawn fades in
when I least expect it.
Where are the books that held me once,
my brave invective,
the pictures forming in the darkroom?
Memory leaves
with her usual lack of meaning,
a darkness with enormous breasts.
The facts open without
a message, as if it were a matter
of style. (In the place of death,
the nurse folds up the linen.)
The constellations disappear,
quarks and quasars
lap at the edges. The universe
grows light, the mist in it
burns off, and I don't know
what emerges. Birdsong.
Something is buried here and it
will rise. Who knows? The angry
catbird wants me gone.

YOU'VE GOT ANOTHER THINK COMING

No, no, hold it, I've had too much already,
Figure my tab, I'm finished, gotta go.
It's midnight. The ship's just easing past the jetty,
And I'm not Socrates, much less Rimbaud.
(When I was young, I thought the French were heady
And had *La Nausée* on my sloshed *bateau*.)
I'd like to drift like stardust on the deep.
But I've got miles to go before I leap.

Oh what the hell, Joe, set up another one,
Like — what is the final cause of being dead?
Why is there being at all instead of none?
Am I awake, like Gregor on his bed,
Or is there nothing new under the sun?
These questions hang like something made of lead,
An anchor going down — slowly, slowly.
I'll never plumb the depths! — or love you wholly,

Sweetheart. Joe, see what that lady's thinking.
Is she the Muse? My spouse? A feminist?
She seems to be staring at me, straight, unblinking,
Maybe enthralled with me, or maybe pissed.
What does it mean, this linking and unlinking
Across great distance? Does she even exist?
(Now there's a think that's been around so long
It's like a golden-oldie jukebox song.)

She gives me fever. So give me penicillin.
Joe, I've been through the mill, from the pre-Socratic
Dam builders to Wittgenstein and Dylan.
I've even ruminated on ecstatic
Links with God, but like some Blakean villain,
Mork or whoever, forged a world so static,
That nothing lived in it. Except, alas,
For me. I longed for sacraments. For mass.

Another thaw. The icy water stuns
The nerves of my hand, pauses, plunges through
The spillway to the pond where mayfly duns
Blink open on the surface, just a few —
Little things, little things, bear scat, axions,
Wood ducks or wood frogs quacking in the slough,
A reddish vapor over the maple limbs,
The viruses of childhood, and its hymns.

What does *what* mean? It means I'm dry, Joe,
Dry as the land surrounding the Euphrates
With all its endless warfare. That being so,
Bring me and the lovely — whoops, I see the lady's
Gone. Yet I remember her: the glow
Of her eyes, like someone just come up from Hades,
Who saw me with my mind tied up in knots
And loved me till I had no other thoughts.

LEAVING LITTLE TO CHANCE

Everything cooking, everything going,
a juggling act, a balance between
nothing and burning, something or other
keeping it going, always in motion,
chopping, splitting, blending,
doing, undoing, whisks and spoons
rattling like crazy, spatulas
scraping, everything cooking,
eggs and bacon, burgers and fries,
corned beef and cabbage, pasta
al dente, broiled bluefish,
brains à la York, brioches, butterscotch,
chicken timbales, cucumber soup,
cauldrons simmering, steaming,
everything cooking, someone or other
leaving nothing alone, rushing
from cupboard to counter to stove,
making sure that everything's cooking,
even the coffee perking for later,
for leisure, the vigil lights of the burners
glowing, everything cooking,
loaf cakes, layer cakes, pound cakes,
Yorkshire pudding, quiche Lorraine,
blanquette de veau, coquilles St. Jacques
Derridá, duxelles, halibut, hare
(hash for tomorrow), peas and carrots,
garbanzos and peppers, pineapple popcorn,
porcupine, mei goo gai pan,
everything cooking, everything sizzling,
all systems go, adrenalin,
pistons, turbines, Mount
St. Helens, someone or other

forgetting the potholder, cursing
the wondrous idea that everything's cooking,
ragout and rarebit, rhubarb and rice,
Brunswick stew, shellfish and Sauternes,
soufflé and silence, spinach and squash,
turtles and tongue, biscuit tortoni,
pilaf, fritters, gnocchi,
everything cooking, something lost
in commotion, something falling apart
like an old cobweb, something or other
unavailable for sweet
or terrible surprises —
the riddle of the Märchen,
the book of hours, bloodlight, even
those wallowings, those sobs
in a single place, those mysteries
of doing nothing.

IT DOESN'T ADD UP

How paltry life seems: mine, yours,
The mailman's, hapless agitated dross
Dividing, filling wombs and sewers,
Nailed and wriggling on a cross,

Sprayed as a pest at country clubs,
Flapping, drowning, standing tall,
Marching to Popes or Beelzebubs,
Flipped on a grill, gunned down at a mall —

So what's the choice? Eat or be eaten.
The earth itself is a rich stew,
A hot cauldron to toss the meat in.
Meaning, the mailman. Me. You.

As if inclined to slash their wrists,
Many have brooded thus, including
(*Ubi sunt?*) the Modernists.
It's paltry, too, all this brooding.

My favorite Modernist is Hardy.
He knew what "hap" meant. Also "twain"
Converging, as when, doing 40,
Making a poem in my brain

(This one, as it happens), giving
Little heed to nature, I catch,
From my eye's corner, something living
Dart from the woods and into the path

Of my car — "Damn it!" — and disappear.
I swerve, slam on the brakes, stall,

Get out and hurry back to where
It may not have happened, a green wall:

But there it lies on the asphalt, furry,
Soft and limp like a child's beanbag,
A chipmunk, no longer in a hurry,
A chance occurrence without meaning,

Only a dot of red on its snout
To show that this is meat to please
An avid crow. Meanwhile, my route
Proceeds, between the walls of trees.

How paltry life seems, yours, mine,
This poem's, if it has any,
The snap and crackle of every line
Seeming to *fizzle* out, like static.

A poem *doesn't* live, not really.
It has no eyes, no spine, no liver.
What you suppose is a poem's feeling
Isn't, though it last forever.

Feelings don't. I think of my father,
Clutching my hand, a paltry thing
Like a chipmunk, a feeling, just another
Death. So. Why this lingering?

ONE FOOT IN THE GRAVE

Mehr Licht! Mehr Licht!

Dragging it around
like a bear trap,
limping with an ugly,
unpredictable lurch
like the club-footed
heir apparent,
I am still
a creature in the world.

Sometimes, driving home
at night, maybe after
a couple of beers,
free at last of the earth's
pull, my car immense
with Bach, I am
deep, like a well
that plumbs the universe.

Daylight, glaring,
gets thick again with work.
I swear, caught up in it,
snagged by a million
tiny snares like some
poor soul in a masterpiece
by Bosch, all my struggles
making things worse,

or like a B movie
villain, sinking
in what I thought was solid
ground: the years.

Only my hand
is up as if I had
a question. And the living
light above me blurs.

FACING THE MUSIC

— for Alex

It starts like a whisper in your head,
Or a low humming, distant hooting,
A barred owl, chorus frogs in March,
A dark horizon line of pines
Where a tune is hovering in the air,
Simple, available, that fills
    Your being, then more of you,
Flowing like water through a fish's gills.

Then it begins to throb, to swell,
To form itself in lines and layers,
Woodwinds, brass, continuo,
The choir in complex harmony,
Cantatas, masses, simple prayers
A holy challenge! And so you keep
    To the stepping stones of Bach,
A way over the water, which is deep.

And it swells some more, cracking, uncoiling,
Opening to the abyss of self;
The strings intensify, the horns
Announce the engulfing wave of Frühling:
Mahler's languid sprawl, tumescent
Neuroses — nostalgia for the past,
    Spring flowers, children, the voice
That rang so pure for God, that didn't last.

Sad, sad. And finally, irritating,
A nagging, techno throb, not even
The steady tomtom of desire,

More like a jingle on TV
Drilling you to be a buyer
Of gum, cosmetics, beer that's made
        From Rocky Mountain water.
So you stand in line, weary, if unafraid.

Still, the sadness stays, a long
Liturgical chant, the vigil lights
Flickering on the stove at midnight,
Staccato of coughing from the bedroom,
Drained blue arteries of trees
In the kitchen windows. Here where you putter,
        Water steams away
From the kettle. The house is thick with cold, dark matter.

Facing the music must be like —
Rethinking your life perhaps? (Breaking
The old, shellac records over
Your husband's head!) The music's under
A trapdoor, swollen shut. (The husband
Walks in water, casting a fly,
        Finding it hard to believe
That a whole ocean could at last go dry.)

TALKING TO HEAR MY HEAD RATTLE

As if something inside is loose,
a belt, a bearing, a dozen bolts,
a couple of million brain cells —
what if someone profound, like God
or Miss Scolla in the fourth grade,
were listening to this racket?

Who cares, when nothing's working?
I think it means I'm giving up the ghost,
something making me jittery,
something suddenly shooting up my spine
like a chimney fire — something about
childhood, the prison that never knew me.

Maybe it's notes from underground,
drills probing the mine, the noise of the earth-shaker,
the rumbling, the preparation, the new me
about to erupt — and maybe not,
maybe it's just my Muse with her maracas,
her tall hat full of bananas.

Something, I say, is loose,
something truer than art — yes! — the blown gasket
between the brain's two halves,
the clean connection that should let me sing
the Song of Myself
so the world out there can understand it.

FAMOUS LAST WORDS

Time to go, be done, like a frozen lake
Becoming slush in August, like a shelf
Of *National Geographics*, like a fruitcake,
Like LPs, like playing with oneself.
Time to present the ultimate one-liner,
To whisper my confession to the priest,
To sink into corruption and decline
Like the Roman empire — to be, at last, a beast,
Food for worms, and hold the literature!
Time to cut out the idle, empty talk,
The daily lack of meaning and its jury.
Time to catch a thermal like a hawk
At the equinox. Time to be on my way.
Time to screech whatever I have to say.

BEYOND BELIEF

There is a town in the desert without flags,
Without signs, without even graffiti,
Without lights except for constellations
To show you where you are, "middle of nowhere,"
As they say, those quaint geographers
Who once assured you there was nothing there.
But you knew better, even then. You knew
That shimmering mirage on the horizon
Was something burning.
               All night long, the wind
Howls down from the mountain passes, driving dust
That fills the air, blurring moon and stars,
Finding the cracks in so-called solid stuff
Until it settles, somewhere, anywhere,
Like you — if only *you* could be lifted!
                    Briefly
It stops, day dawns petrified, the eastern
Sky turns gunmetal gray, the mountains a kind of
Sickly pink. Slowly the photograph
Develops, the wreckage of the town rises,
A warm breath touches your face, the world
Speeds up, something metallic flaps and bangs,
Tumbleweeds go rolling through the streets
Like human heads, pieces of paper fly.
    A railroad track injects itself into
The town and out, as if afraid,
Furtive. Whatever's left is boarded up,
Shut down. (You once believed that everyone
Was his own lake. And you thought there must be ways
Out of the water.)

Beyond belief, at the rim,
A faded, bubble-headed gas pump stands
Surveying things, like an alien from a saucer:
Blackened, hollow car bodies and trailers,
Buildings with their roofs caved in, charred
Studs and shingles, a froth of smells, burnt
Rubber, plastic, horsehair furniture-stuffing,
Creosote, bile, grease, a fifty-five-
Gallon drum that still holds something dreadful.
You know this place: it's all those years of seeking
The self in its gilded frame.
                              Surely, you say,
Something else exists beyond belief,
No one thinks that this is the way things are,
Everyone knows there's "real life," even here,
Like — who knows? — beyond that rock, a sidewinder
Unwinding, sand-colored, seeking body heat,
Like yours.
                  A hummock of tires looms over
The scattered TV sets with bashed-in tubes,
Defunct appliances, rusty cans, shards
Of vinyl records, bedsprings, bones, a clock,
A woman's slip that floats by in the wind,
The dust, the flying scraps of paper, pages
From calendars and comics, tacky novels,
Literary stuff (*Perspective, kayak*),
Forgotten letters, someone's stamp collection
Freed, unhinged, whirling about, bits of
Rhodesia, *Deutsches Reich*, United States —
Words! Who could make choices here? The wind
Plays itself, over and over, like a jukebox
Honky-tonking the same, obsessive tune,
Someone's reminder, someone's sense of loss.

        Beyond belief is you, yes, the middle
Of nowhere, almost at home there, too, as if
You had built it, though you can't help looking back
To the place you longed to leave.
                                        Beyond belief
There is a roaring torrent. It is what is,
Your life, the dream of water going elsewhere.

GONE HAYWIRE

. . . the Lord of hosts has a day against all that is proud and
lofty, against all that is lifted up and high, against all the
cedars of Lebanon, lofty and lifted up; and against all the
oaks of Bashan; against all the high mountains, and against
all the lofty hills; against every high tower, and against
every fortified wall. . . .
> —Isaiah 2:12-15

. . . young men must live.
> —Falstaff, in *1 Henry IV*, 2.2

1.
His revelation: whatever blood-light the Lord
demanded of my son that night,
it came out ragged, full of holes, the message
mangled like road kill. He was beyond
fear, flapping like his totem eagle over
the dark streets.
                    Held down
on the gurney by the cops, he was read
the fact of the needle, and he
curled up like a child
and fell asleep.

2.
A satori, as he called it, had awakened
him from fear.
He had stayed locked in for days
with the handwriting on the wall (his own

tormented graffiti),
his high-rise apartment totally trashed,
moldy dishes, broken
refrigerator, clothes and spilled containers
strewn on the floor.
                          Meanwhile,
someone was right outside
in the hallway, smoking,
now and then
slipping pieces of paper
under the door.

3.
His satori also opened for him
a prodigious vision:
the Great Millennial Flood brought on by global warming,
the last survivors clinging to
the immense antennae on the World Trade Center towers,
great white sharks circling in their element,
picking people off
as the heaving waters rose even higher.

4.
This was before the summer of the sharks,
the turning of the Twin Towers into
ashes and dust,
in the first year of the honest-to-God
millennium, 2001,
reams of paper flying out
against the black smoke.

5.
My son, my son! his voice ranting
in the wilderness of Newark in the warm
(global warming!) winter of 1999,
stalking the streets, pigeon-holing

panhandlers and crackheads, proclaiming
the baptism of fire and the sword
when all they wanted was bread, man,
bread. "We are all native Americans!"
he shouted, grabbing them by their
hands, their arms, or even (in my case)
the shirt collar,
twisting it in a way that was
foreign, as if I were a prisoner of war.
"Shut up!
Shut up! You always tell me
I don't listen!"

6.
Two years before
the summer of the sharks, the fall
of the Temple of Mammon, the Great Satan,
container for the thing contained,
hearts, bones,
incessant flesh that struggled to get out,
container for the thing contained.

7.
Tower of Babel, Twin Towers,
transcendent latticework
of glass and steel, sinking,
sunk. Eerie, like trying to imagine
a black hole.

8. *A survivor*
"Can you see sky?"

9.
The summer of the shark,
2001—how paltry

this seems now! The uncle
pulling his nephew's arm
from the bull shark's gullet, a mere
curiosity among so many body parts.
Nature's revenge,
my son predicted.
Light a votive candle for them.

10. *The son*
"I had the bandana around my neck
and my face all smudged with black like a
working-class terrorist. I saw
on the street that everyone
was wearing a bandana; girls
would be wearing white, while guys
were wearing red — yuppies, homies,
whoever. I'd seen all these people
before. I'd forgotten. And then
the phone rang in a booth I just
happened to be passing, and sure
enough, when I picked up the receiver,
it was dead.
          "How did you
do it, Dad? How did you
set me up for that one?"

11.
A system
crashes. The so-called
facts — financial reports,
Powerpoint printouts, airline receipts,
telephone bills, employee manuals —
strewn on the ashen streets and sidewalks.

12.
Tower of Babel,
Twin Towers,
information highway
zooming skyward —
"Forgive!" he said.
"Love me!" she said.
The road went up, up and away
into the blue, away
from the flame and smoke. And they
grasped each other's hand
and jumped.

13. *The son*
"I'd been walking around all day.
What happened was, people on the street
kept giving me clues on where to go.
All this is some kind of experiment.
I have an instinct that says Ronnie had
something to do with it. You know
how my mind was all jumbled up?
You thought I had A.D.D., which, I've figured out,
is just some Western trait — anyway,
now my mind is in perfect order."

14.
Tower of Babel, Twin Towers —
the mind can't stand to be everywhere!
Polyglot chaos, dispersal of voices,
tongues of flame, raw sound
like a jet diving.

15.
Ladies and gentlemen,
This is your captain speaking.
It is time to say your prayers.

16.
The tight-lipped spoor of desire,
labels, trade names,
papers and diskettes crammed at the last minute
into a briefcase.
And they all converge, these people who had been
virtual in their cubicles,
and jam the exits. Down they go
and around, down and
around the endless
stairway. "Excuse me."
Making jokes
as the steel buckles.

17.
Swept away,
words in megabytes and flickering pixels,
ghostly paper blown in the firestorm,
banks of data
from which we had tried to fish, while overhead
a lone helicopter without a clue
is flying from tower to tower.

18. *A survivor*
"We could see things twisting
and flipping in the sunlight,
pieces of metal and glass,
and it suddenly dawned on us:
that stuff is coming after us!"

19. *A survivor*
"This thing jumped me! It had enough force
to lift me right out of the water. It felt like
a truck had slammed into me. Then I felt
a compacting squeeze,
an acute burning in my leg."

20.
Skeletal lattice looming behind them,
the great cranes and grapplers lurch over
the smoking debris, poking through
the gobbledegook of steel,
concrete slabs bristling with rebar,
shards of glass, pulverized sheetrock,
tangled skeins of red cable —
as if death were a great
Dumpster.
                    Count!
Count them. How many body bags
will not be needed?

21. *A survivor*
"We all washed out our
mouths. You'd be amazed
at what came out, at what was
plugged up our noses and ears and in
the backs of our throats."

22.
The "wacko ward," as he calls it,
nurses, orderlies,
the feeling of being in
a submarine. We bring him
a "Care package" from Burger King,
find our niche in the cramped
visitors' room. He's cranky,
irritable, wants out, but even more,
a cigarette. "Come on,
smuggle some in for me, will you?"
His t-shirt says "The Casualties,"
the name of a punk band.
He paces, swears, cracks

his knuckles. No more visions,
no satori, now he's just
one of the grey people, all burnt out,
a shade to bring gifts to.

23.
Blahblahblah.
The dead don't mutter.
The dead don't dance in the mosh pit
and play loud music.
The dead don't fuss and fart
and rant in the streets
or in my house. And of course:
"... none do there, I think, embrace."
(The irony waves bye-bye
and jumps, like Berryman,
but doesn't die like him. Oh no!)
Let me make one thing
perfectly clear:
This was supposed to be a poem
about a sick young man
living on his own in a "blighted city"
where he had what's called a "nervous breakdown."
(Words elude me.)
His prodigious vision was right out of an artless
disaster film.
No historical value here,
no event.
Maybe my heart imploded, that's all.
Maybe I'm heartless.

24.
Terror and pity.
I'm not the Tin Man, no,
more like Batman, high above
Gotham, brooding over

Ground Zero.
Unreal city! Unreal city!

25.
"I don't need this," my son says
through his teeth. "I don't need this. I can't
find my fucking cap." And I can feel the knot
tighten. He paces, picks up magazines, hymn books,
starts flinging the stuff about. What next?
Fist through the wallboard? A window?
"Son, wait," I say. "Fuck you,
old man. You wuss. You sorry
piece of shit." Later, he comes back
weeping, hugging me, begging
forgiveness. "I can't live like this,"
my wife says. I turn cold,
delete myself. I can't live. I can't
live, say the whole outdoors, the frozen
constellations. The dog
jars me, yanks on her leash
to poke her nose in the roadside leafpile,
sniffing for the perfect place to pee.

Drawings of Faculty Colleagues

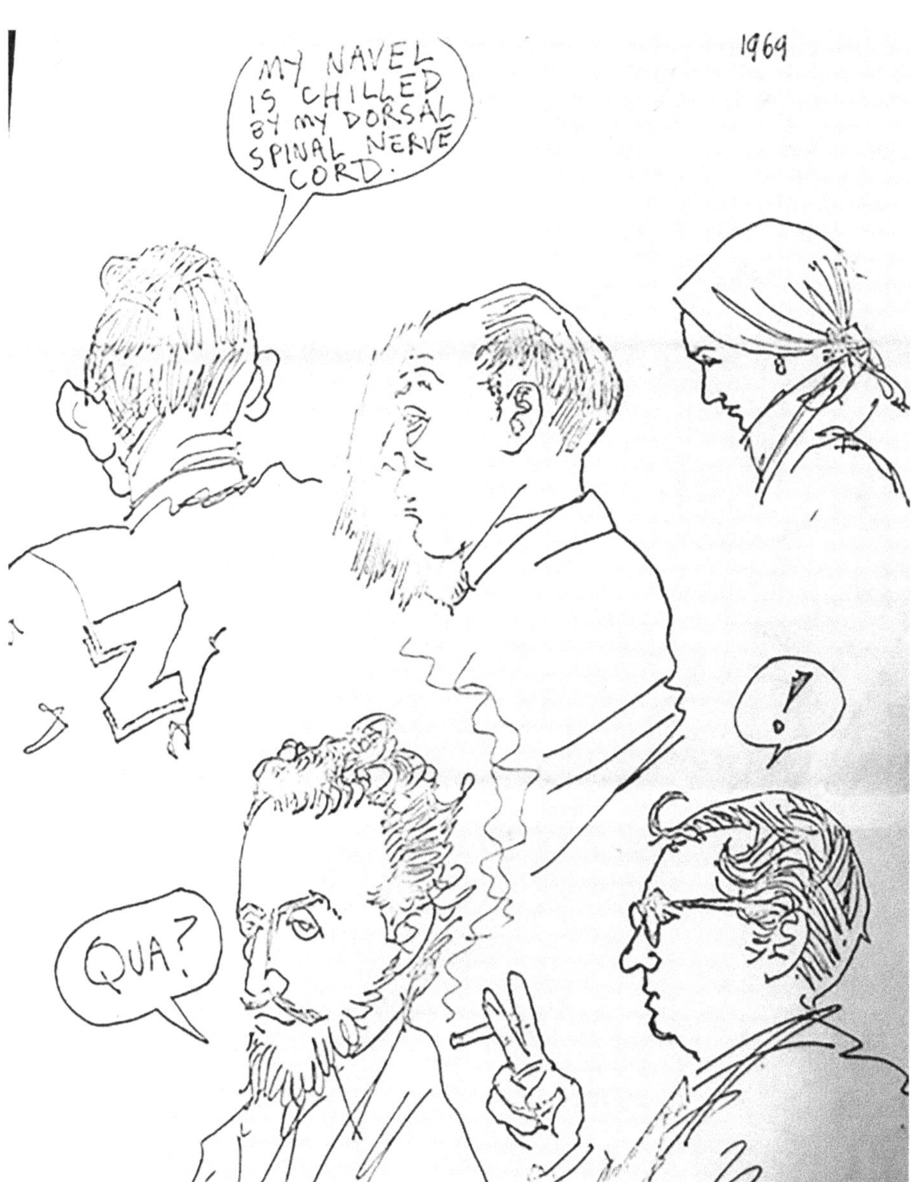
MY NAVEL IS CHILLED BY MY DORSAL SPINAL NERVE CORD.
1969
!
QUA?

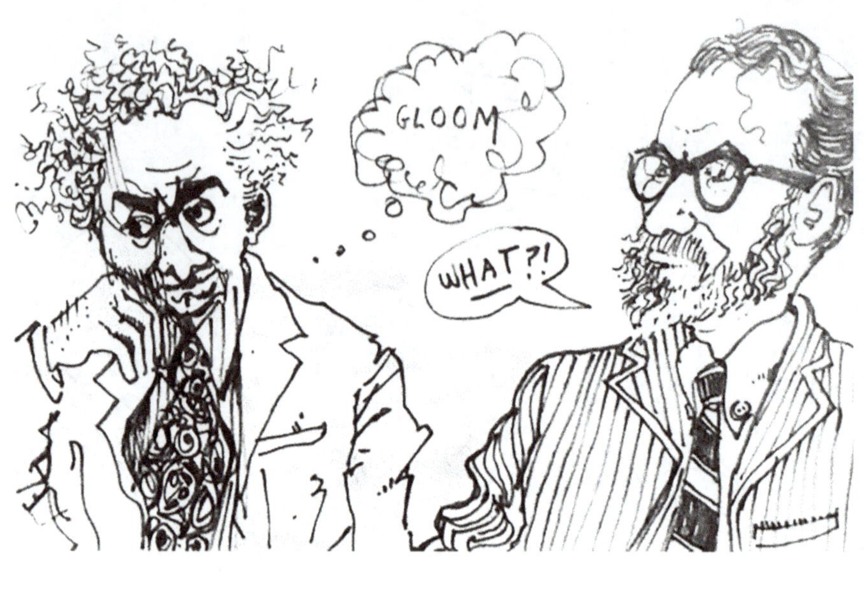

GLOOM
WHAT?!

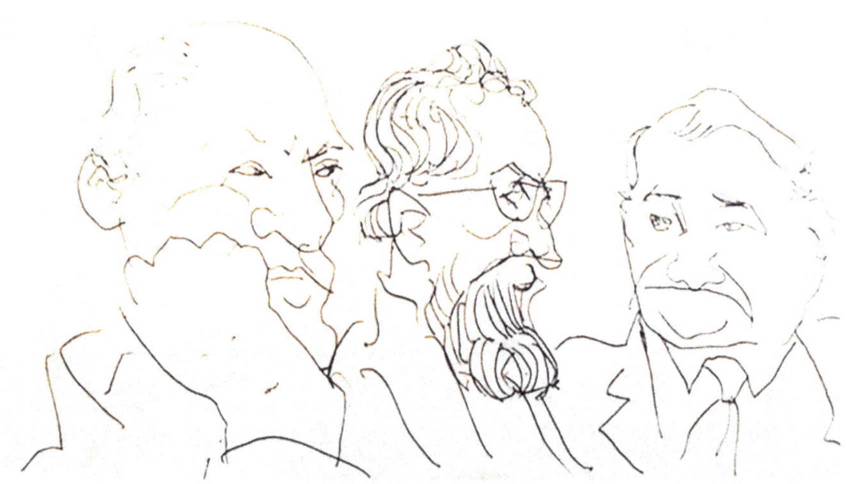

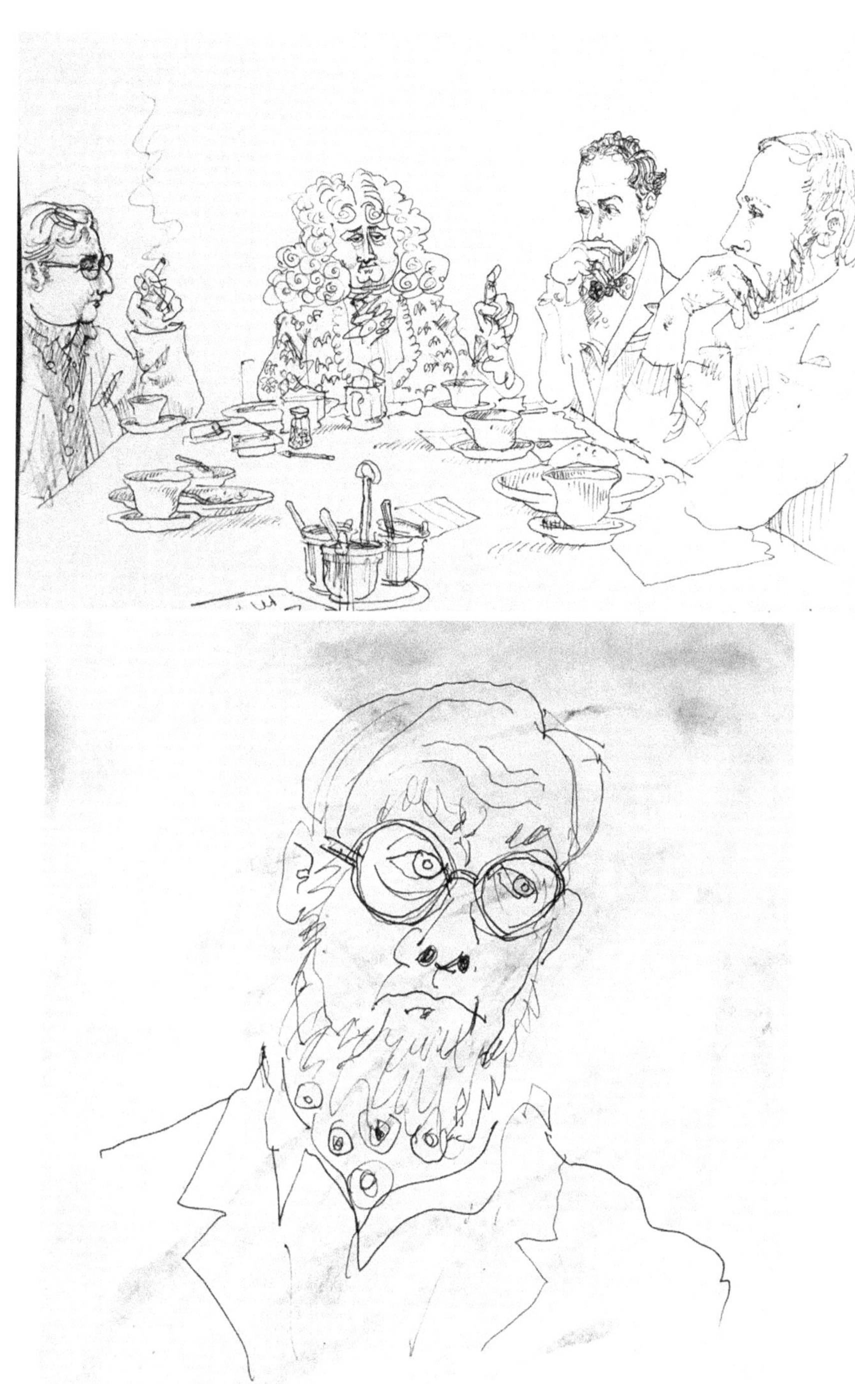

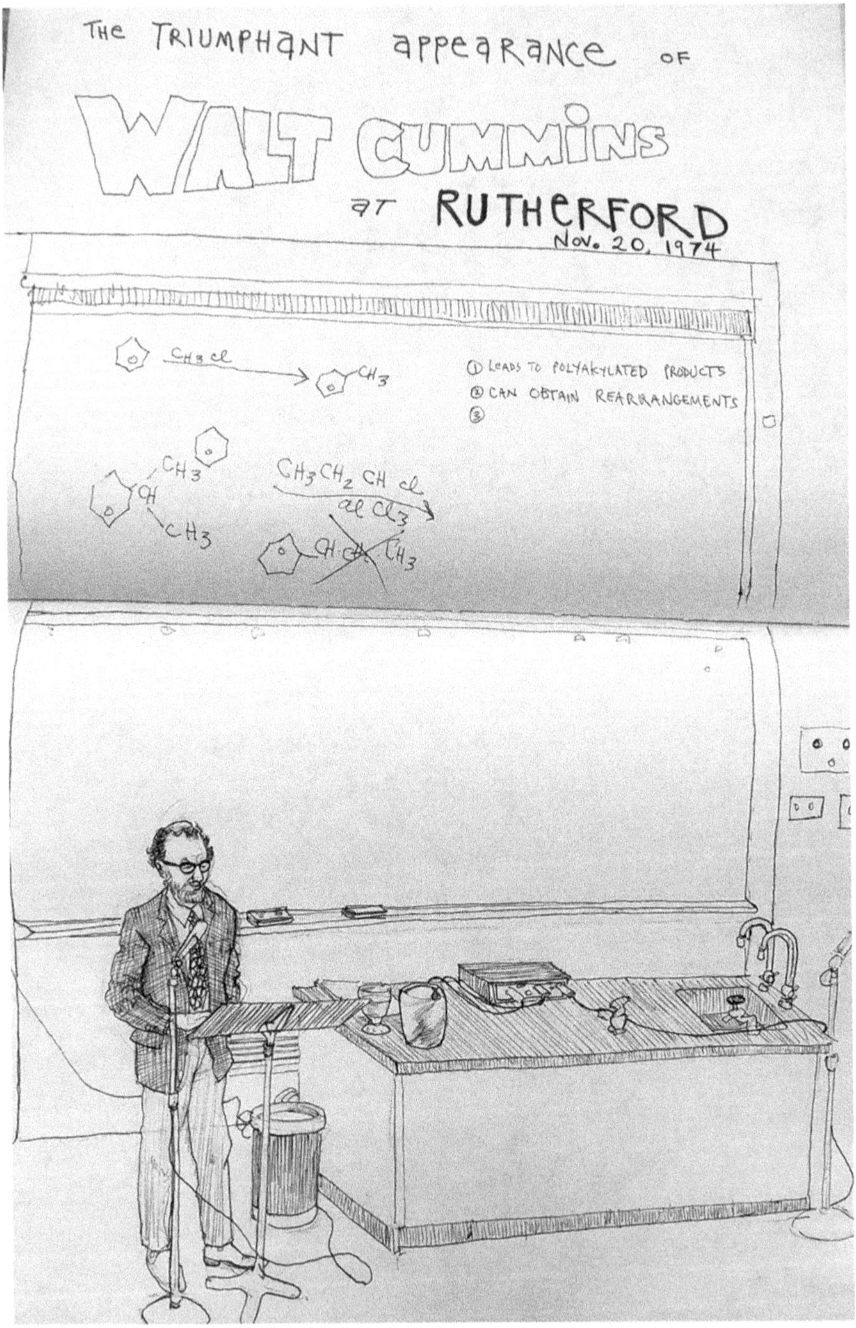

THE TRIUMPHANT APPEARANCE OF
WALT CUMMINS
AT RUTHERFORD
NOV. 20, 1974
CH3 Cl
CH3
① LEADS TO POLYAKYLATED PRODUCTS
② CAN OBTAIN REARRANGEMENTS
③
CH3
CH
CH3
CH3 CH2 CH Cl
Al Cl3
CH CH2 CH3

Uncollected Poems

A POET'S SEVEN DEADLY SINS

1. Boredom

Sometimes, the space you fill
fills you. Empty but not
vast, where even the fury-swarms
go blah. Nothing kills
poetry faster, for even when you snap
to at 3 a.m.,
nothing performs.
Instead, you read
junk, hoping that sleep will suck you
into itself, fat and oral,
a female bag of Freudian clichés.
Meanwhile, the Muse,
with whom you've had a boring quarrel,
snores in the other room,
mere noise.

2. Irritation

"Goddam sombitchin'
idiot asshole!" you proclaim
in your lunar module,
nothing coming through from mission
control, empire starships darting in and
out of your hyperspace,
gridlock of the brain, mnemonic
TV jingles, virus
blowing the microchips and leaving you,
like anyone,
state-of-the-art moronic.
Sealed in here, sealed in at home:
the kids shrieking, banging
into your privates, wife with her nagging
money worries, dog patiently
barking from behind the dead piano.
Things happen, heaps of clutter,
junk mail, dirty dishes that reproduce
on the kitchen counter, toys sown on the carpet:
booby traps for insomniac bare feet.
Handles that come off in your hand,
clothes that shrug off their hangers,
potholes, open drawers, corners
of things to intercept you, SHIT! The Muse
a pain in the ass like everything,
one more item on a crowded list
"Goddam bitch . . . !"
Your passion is a spook, a limbo
lunatic, an apparition
like the moon itself, silvery, static
in the simmering fumes
above the traffic.

3. Contempt

Surveying the fields of praise
from the last pew, you see
the cropped necks, the casual coifs,
the bright silk scarves,
solids, stripes, bleeding madras,
rising, falling. The plangent
organ leads them in
the same Victorian hymns that sat
on your youth like the queen
sans miracle, sans sense of sin.
Murmurs, the flipping pages of the text,
the soul raised in the sermon like the ghastly
Lazarus: it enters your combed head
which had been drifting in contempt
of yuppies, joggers herded by Walkman,
MBAs with their sweet Mercedes.
Where now your callow
railing against the bourgeoisie,
your weighted beads, soles of your feet,
the blue lobster on its leash? You
waving your manifesto like a cock
in their pink faces, which you can't see?
Ah, there's nothing new
under the sun to mortify their ladies!
"God is dead!" would hardly shock
even that nun, even screamed from the pulpit.
You have nothing to say to them.
Silence. Regard them down the rows of pews.
Sans immortality. Sans muse.

4. Lust

Those lurking poets, those
heated brains, those obscene callers who refuse
to say what they mean, those gate
crashers, grave robbers,
morticians of the Muse —
oh how they love to penetrate!
It's not enough
being a Workshop Poet, is it?
Then let us go and make our visit:
agents bidding to make your book
a Major Motion Picture,
groupies screaming at your readings,
scrabbling to tear your clothes off,
you not only richer
but reborn at the lotus center,
fleur du mal
unfolding in the Playboy swimming pool,
voice that howls
in the wilderness of late-night talk shows,
hoarse! raving!
A man, a legend,
In love with the whole world, weeping,
thumping the lectern —
"Ja! Ja! Das Leben!"

5. Work

Show that whore,
Fame, the door.
Be profoundly
alone.
Cultivate the word:
That is
the poet's work.
Fret not
in your narrow cell.
By craft
and sullen art
produce great poems,
one by one,
so when you cast off
for Byzantium
you'll leave behind
your *oeuvre*. As you've
already said,
the Muse is dead, and you
must mourn her by deciding
every word. Don't loafe.
Tell your soul, "Get lost!
Can't you see I'm writing?"

6. Depression

The wife and children disappear
while you're at work, also
the dog, the furniture, the clothes,
only your poetry left behind.
The house is empty and in focus
under the light you've just turned on, quiet
except for katydids outside.
Nothing for dinner, nothing
on television, the walls sliding into
place, the bare windows,
the open doorway and — nothing,
no maple leaf,
nada y nada y pues nada,
zero, zip.
Sometime the emptiness you fill
fills you. Vast,
silent. Nothing's
amusing, epecially
these poems. You want them
wiped out, empty, pure,
like God,
like love,
like Nature —
modern, at last!
But walking in the woods,
fishing, dining,
making love, you
can imagine anything: the child waving
her bloody stumps, the steaming
pile of brains on the pavement, the Indian
with his tongue cut out —
BANG! — a peculiar

smell, acrid like burning
tires. It's got nothing
to do with Nothing, the philosophical
goose egg — Being
gets it big,
the 20th century with its grand
thermonuclear gloom.
There is something though —
Not grief!

The firm commitment of graves, nothing but lumps.

The prose, the pictures in the media.

The child, waving her bloody stumps.

7. Suicide

Suicide,
the bucket, the bullseye,
the end of the affair,
you've had it,
flap flap.
Letting go
of the wrong pitch,
too late,
it's gone, goodbye.
No no,
it's YOU,
the definitive heartthrob,
AIEEE! Sombitch.
O luxurious losses!
Childhood with its intergalactic vistas,
the radio, the comic books,
the teacher with the tight hair,
the goods downtown,
the poet with his song of songs,
the groin that slips out of gear —
Jesus, a long way
down, the mouth,
the gullet, the route
to the underworld, the poet's
spa, the conversation with
your father. Something
completed, something at least
in place — checkmate, ha,
voila!
Obsession or omission,
heavy metal
or mute for honor,

it's the answer
only you can give, looking out
the window: shit,
it's all laborious
out there, Raphael
in the salt mine, so why
go on? Hydrogen vat,
Fourth of July,
hot dogs and watermelon,
bodies on the beach, the night sky
lit up, exposed, the Muse of summer fun,
boring. Like in No. 1.
Fuck 'em. You're closing the lid.
Great, alone
with the Mets in extra innings,
a 13 billionth beer,
a lousy liver and zzzero at the bone.
The Mother of Beauty! —
Here's looking at you, Ma.
Right, sure.
Zzzz. Selah.

HYMN: JESUS H. CHRIST

La blasfemia forma parte de la religion popular.

> —Antonio Machado,
> from *Juan de Mairena*

1.
Kneeling, doing the post-communion prayer with others,
I almost say: ". . . the spiritual food
of the most precious Body and Blood of your Son our Savior
Jesus H. Christ. . . ."
                                    OOPS! It's HIM,
the redneck *Doppelgänger* of our Lord, patron saint
of the pissed off, poking me with his elbow,
good old boy who calms the waters of frustration,
a presence haunting the cluttered garage,
scratching his head, consumed by all the daily things
that need fixing.
                        And here in the church, I feel
a fondness rise in me, like heartburn, thinking how
I've invoked his name in the dark, stumbling over
my son's boots, the cat underfoot, the evil furniture,
my wife's eternally
unfinished sorting, my antique
brain,
my heart in hiding.

2.
How many times in a lifetime of being
irritated have I invoked him?
Jesus H. Christ! in his feed cap
and Sweet-Orr bibs, bringing me back down
to earth, my ass on a barstool —
Why are we here? I sigh, and he guffaws. And so

we sit and drink and chew the fat
and don't much look each other in the eye
but at the TV set above the bar, the tiny
NFL game with the sound turned off —
Is that Tim? kneeling on the sideline
with his flock? I'm feeling mellow
if not saved. "Pass the peanuts," says Jesus H.
"Say, what's that 'H' mean anyhow?" I ask him
out of the blue. "Never you mind," he says.
"Pete, let's have two more." "Well then,
let me guess. I bet it's 'Henry,' Everyman,
like in *The Dream Songs*." "Nope," he says.
"Boy, you sure do think you're smart, don'tcha? Which
reminds me," and he starts to tell the one
about the hooker and the Pharisee.
"Is it Hosea?" I ask. "I believe you had one a those
somewhere back in the family tree."
"Nope," he says, and raises a fresh,
sparkling, amber glass
and puts it in my hand. "Take,"
he says. "Drink up.
Go on now, be
a fisher of fish."

3.
Jesus H. Christ! That silly name,
reductio ad absurdum of the solemn,
not in vain — no! It is the Word
as self-expression, a release
like air from a tire - slow down!
I call upon it when I'm overwhelmed
by trivial happenstance, all those tiny
things of the world crawling over me
and biting.
          Jesus H. Christ, my cry
in the wilderness, my S.O.P. ejaculation

whenever I bark my shin, mislay my glasses,
spill my coffee, find myself
boxed-in by rush-hour traffic. Proclaimer of
the broken fingernail, the bad-hair day, the humdrum
marriage, dogshit on the sole, empty
IRS forms, clogged pipes — O friend, o JHC,
protector not of losers (our Lord looks after them),
but of the inadequate, the normal, those who lack
and don't especially want love.
                                        There is
no mission, no messianic blood,
no destiny, no way
to bear one's own cross, lost
as it is in all this junk, this cluttered garage, this raging
heart of a would-be fisherman, tangled up
in monofilament line. Who
will release him? Who will reveal to him
the True Name, plain as day?

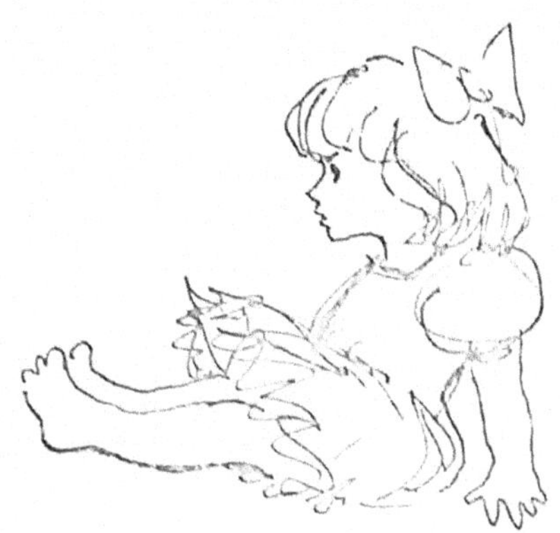

Toes are stranger than rabbits
and wiggle around like a nose,
But they grow as familiar as habits—
Those tiny, unusual toes!

Toes are apart, yet together,
each with its own little nail,
You can tickle the toes with a feather,
or swish them around in a pail.

A toe isn't much like a parrot
for I've never found one that talks
They're not good to eat, like a carrot,
but fine for filling up socks.

Toes are as useful as mother
for learning to count over ten,
But washing between them's a bother,
and I'll never do it again.

Errors, Ideas, Edits

WILLIAM ZANDER

The broad-wingeds rise and circle on the thermal,
Weightless beings, as if they lived on air
As mortals do on food. Commingling, quarreling
Like the Corinthians, they let you see them
for a while, then fall away into space,
One more finicky dream, unanswered prayer.
But then, *you're* the philosopher, the kind
that invented weightlessness, for what it's worth.
You didn't invent these hawks. Some will come back
In spring, feathers ragged from molt and travel,
Drop from the sky, pierce the treetops, zigzag
Through them, see the snake exactly, see
The stones, the duff, the ground that gave them birth.

68

Too much galagaging
wandering lonely
as a cloud.

Bite your tongue,
corrupt granddaughter
B/Y/T w/o keys! in the presence
of your principal
your tired father,
shuffling in from
the graveyard shift.
BYT when you think
you know,
BYT, even though
you know the answer,
Don't let your face
w darkness light up
that engaged
sense of profundity
that communicates
wags even when
you bite your tongue.
Be kind in the
presence of bedsores,
sleeplessness,
exzema,
the presence of . . .

BYT when you're feeling
~~tired~~ [tiny] lucky
  almost blank.
~~and to make up for it~~
~~feel the need to battle~~
  slip between the
    cracks of the crowd
+ get out ~~past~~ fast.
    ~~to~~ Walk a
      long way in the
        cold.
Bite your tongue for the
    witty comeback
that falls [flat]
    + ~~flaunt~~ up +
      stop
      theatrically down
on the ground.
    BYT for the saving
grace.
    BYT till the tip
falls off.
    flies out like a
      Heimlich[er] missile

Talk Is Cheap

like the Motel Algarabía. I mean, you know?
like when you're humming along the two-lane highway
through those humped, golden hills, doing maybe
80, middle of nowhere, yackety-yakking
with whoever, nothing to look at all around except,
beyond the right-of-way, some tangled barbed wire,
rusted harrows and threshers, and high above
the drought-tormented landscape, a red-tailed hawk,
power-transmission lines strung out forever on
their towers of silence. And so you talk,
hardly stopping to catch your breath.
                                  Suddenly
dusk comes down like a lid, the windows cloud up,
you flip on the headlights, the defroster, the radio
without missing a beat, until the car
lurches, UMPH, throwing you forward, veers to the shoulder —
and it looks as if you will have to shut up at last
about Jen and her medieval hang-ups.
                                  The engine gasps
like an enemy being strangled. Stops. "Shit. I can't
believe this is happening," you say. "Max,
that son of a bitch, he's the one who talked me into
taking this god-forsaken. . . . Hey, turn that down,
will you? Sure, I like it too, but. . . . What's that

up ahead? Now? Perhaps whither?"
                                        Something

appears in the gloom. (Yes, it's the old story,

you have dreamt it for five million years.) Now

you see it's a white building, maybe maybe

shining like a UFO. And hanging from

a kind of gallows, a pale neon sign, blinking

VACANCY, over and over.
                                        Darkly, you lean toward

your companion. "It's a motel," you say. "Are you awake?

Or have I talked you to death?" Let her sleep,

let the pieces of the mosaic (what mosaic?)

fall into place. Open the door, get out, close it gently,

cross the highway, push that across its crossbars

between two keys, unshaven palms in a line-up

door of frosted glass. What lies within? ?

                                        What

indeed? In fact, what does it mean? Why are you here

at all? And what

do you matter to yourself, what old man's

imprecations, mumblings without music? And why

do innocents suffer, why

have you come so far, changing form and floating

a real presence, your laughter hollow

as if from a catacomb? Fool! You've never waited

for an answer.

                    Nothing. Nothing but narrative.

· ·

Behold: an art-deco reception desk unfolds,

and on a banner in red Day-Glo letters

hung on the arch above it.

Story
"The Praise of Folly"

THE PRAISE OF FOLLY

"Tell it like it was," says Walt Cummins, my artistic conscience.

He means this story. You see, I'd been browsing around for a character to fit Cotton Combs, a coat with a little padding, something to thicken him up a bit. As it is, he's a bit ghostly, lurking in white long johns, scratching his balls. Assuming there was anything much to know, I didn't know Cotton at all. So I'd been thinking about the fictional padding, motivation, internal conflicts, &c., till Walt says, "Tell it like it was," adding the hip "baby" to show he isn't serious.

Well, neither am I, so I will. I'll start at the University of Missouri, where I was a journalism student in the late fifties. Originally, I had been an art major, but reneged as soon as it became clear to me how artists were supposed to live — cold-water lofts in the Village and all that. My dreams, for some reason, centered on a Chris-Craft cabin cruiser and debauched wanderings up and down the Gulf of California. I was very romantic.

I was also in-love, but that wasn't so important. All my dreams centered on that cabin cruiser. Why go to college at all, except to get a good job when you get out? Thus I reasoned to myself and others, over beers and Polish sausage at the Stein Club.

In 1908, Walter Williams founded the world's first school of journalism at M.U., and it was still considered one of the best, at least by the staff. They really laid it on the line there. I remember once when a representative from the D'arcy Advertising Agency in St. Louis appeared as a guest speaker. He showed us some ads and spoke of one, something to do with soap I think, as "schlocky but effective." A question regarding this was on the final exam.

So I was learning a lot of valuable things.

Elsewhere, I was doing cartoons for *Showme*, the campus humor rag (banned twice while I was there, of which I was not a little proud), and chug-a-lugging with my fraternity brothers.

"SO HERE COMES ANOTHER VERSE THAT'S WORSE

THAN THE OTHER VERSE," we sang every weekend in our basement, equipped with intercom and hollow-seated benches in case of a raid. Someone would start throwing beer cans and Mud, our Weimaraner mascot, was made to retrieve them, receiving as a reward a saucer of beer. "Ha, ha," we laughed. Then my girl and I would go into the other room, which was relatively dark, to dance and do a little public necking.

One of my best pals in the fraternity was Rick Ryan, who was majoring in art education. I still see him occasionally and kid him about his name; it's right out of a comic book, the kind we both learned to draw from when we were kids. Rick and I used to mess around with his tape recorder, doing Bob and Ray-type routines. Rick had real wit, the first I'd encountered outside of some professors. He knew how to be subtle and tried to get me to be too. "Poor," he'd say matter-of-factly, after I'd just put some *Mad*-magazine grotesquerie on the tape.

Unless he was doing a tape, Ryan always seemed to be sleeping. He was only vaguely involved in the fraternity. His clothing was nondescript, unlike the aggressively ivy-league outfits of others. He had medium-long brown hair, parted at the side and combed straight over like Will Rogers, and a jutting jaw with a persistent five-o'clock shadow. "Poor," he'd say in chapter meetings, if he was awake.

One winter night I returned to the house after a date and heard the tape-recorder going in his room. I walked right in; you can't expect privacy in a frat house. I was startled by an apparition in white who sat on a bottom bunk. Ryan was on top, his back against the wall, a can of beer in his hand.

"This is Cotton Combs," he announced. "He's an artist and he's going to Europe."

The apparition saluted like a soldier, without getting up. The white came from three sources:

1. a suit of long winter underwear, the likes of which I'd never seen before.

2. a whitish-blond crewcut.

3. teeth.

"Howdy," said Cotton.

I opened a beer and we listened to the end of the tape. Cotton guffawed every so often.

"You got an extra bed, don't you?" Ryan asked me. "His roommate was expelled for stealing books and selling them to the bookstore," he explained to Cotton.

"Now he's got a job with Dun & Bradstreet," I said.

"He was house manager too," said Ryan. "Want another beer?"

"At least. And flip the tape."

Cotton just grinned and guffawed and scratched himself. I don't remember him saying another word as we sat there drinking beer and listening to tapes.

Sometime or other I learned he was from Smithville, Ryan's hometown. Smithville is in Clay County, Missouri, about 17 miles from North Kansas City. It's in the same county with Kearney (where Jesse James was born) and colorful places like Roosterville and Paradise. It's a rural community, pop. maybe 1200, on the Little Platte River.

Sometimes we wonder what it's all about, what we're doing here and why. But I was unprepared for Cotton's question as he crawled, in his union suit, into the top bunk in my room and I doused the light.

"You believe in God?" he asked, as the room settled into predawn dimness.

"I don't think so," I said.

"Me neither."

Pretty soon he was snoring .

Cotton had cleared out before I awoke at noon.

For the rest of my days at M.U., the apparition was out-of-sight, out-of-mind. Ryan graduated in January and moved to Kansas City. There was nothing much to do but concentrate on that diploma; I still had visions of the cabin cruiser and free-love on the gulf. The fact that I was getting married next summer didn't seem to blur it.

For next summer was associated in my mind with the cabin cruiser; it was suddenly the place to be, a horizon I looked upon with wild surmise. "I'm so excited," I wrote in a letter to Ryan, "that when I shit the turds come out in hard little balls and ricochet around the toilet bowl."

I think my marriage was the least of it. First of all, I was graduating, at long last getting away from the drabness of J School. Secondly, I was moving to K.C., where Ryan and I could continue our beer drinking and tape sessions as if nothing had happened. Thirdly, I already had a job, a better one than I could have hoped for, with Hallmark Contemporary Cards, the funny ones. My dad, who owned the biggest retail greeting-card outlet in the Midwest, had got my foot in the door. It was marvelous, consider; I had believed that the only way to get the cabin cruiser was to give up, at least to some extent, "creativity." But this could never happen at Hallmark.

The girl I was marrying was an old flame. We'd begun dating in high school in Omaha and, despite sporadic fights and breakups, she'd followed me to Missouri to enroll at Stephens College. All is vanity, saith the preacher, and "True Love" is the greatest vanity of all, the assumption that God will see to it that two people "are meant for each other." Dear girl, we based everything on that assumption. Years later and miles away we were divorced, but then we were young and in love, sure that everything could be settled by a wedding — a big one, she insisted, despite my Bohemian sneers.

So we kissed goodbye the weekend of my graduation, she to go to Omaha and help our parents set the ceremonial stage, I to go to K.C. and find an apartment and start work. The first thing I did when I got there was call Ryan.

"Getting any?" I asked him.

Enough, he told me. We did a Bob-and-Ray routine over the phone. He had a lot of things to show me, he said, some new paintings. It's funny, I knew Ryan more as a recording than a graphic artist at school. He kept most of his paintings and drawings in his locker in the art building.

"Cotton's back and we're having a show at the Blue Springs Shopping Center next week," he said.

"Cotton?"

"Sure, you know, the guy from Smithville. He 's been to Europe."

It wasn't till Ryan mentioned the long johns that I caught on.

We arranged to meet at Kelly's. Kelly's, formally known as the Westport Inn, is the best bar in town and incredibly Irish. It's in the oldest building still standing in K.C., or so says a plaque outside. Westport was once a separate town, begun by a man named McCoy, who opened a store there in 1832. For a while it thrived, what is now Kansas City being known as Westport Landing. But in 1849, an epidemic of Asiatic cholera almost ruined Westport, and before the turn of the century, the City of Kansas had absorbed it. I don't know why I mention this, except as an instance of the irony of fate.

Rick and Cotton were already tucked away in a booth near the front when I got there . It was a hot muggy day, and Kelly's isn't air-conditioned, so I sweated and put down beers like a champ while we talked. Ryan was his usual easy-going, ironic self, despite an evident enthusiasm for the glories of K.C. as opposed to M.U.; he looked comfortable in a yellow polo shirt and khakis. Cotton, for some reason, was in a blue gabardine suit and tie, wrinkled with humidity but stiff and formal in some fundamentalist way, like the country people in Walker Evans' photographs. Round shouldered, slightly pudgy, red-faced and hook-nosed under the short crop of blondish hair, he seemed to be a kind of redneck cherub, consciously stiff on his bench while others floated around.

Ryan drawled on easily about last winter and spring, how he'd done some sort of assistant teaching at the big K.C. high school and was to take over the art classes from a little old lady, who was retiring, next fall. Poor old lady. She'd come into class with all sorts of creative projects.

"But what these kids do, it's like when we were in high school, remember?" Ryan said. "Every kid has something he draws over and over, something he likes. Like most of the girls draw horses, a couple do beauty queens in big puffy formals at the prom. Most of the guys do mechanical drawings of cars, one does wild west and civil war scenes with a croquil pen — real detailed, you know, with CSA on the belts, and a lot of cross-hatching."

"I remember," I said, blinking against the beer and humidity.

"Yeah, well the old lady brings in these projects, like 'expressing your inner emotions on paper' while she plays Tchaikovsky's Fifth Symphony on a record player. And what do the kids draw?"

"What?"

Horses, girls in formals at the prom" — and I joined him so we finished the sentence in chorus "cars, and civil war scenes."

As for the summer, Ryan was taking it easy, living with his mother in North K.C., dating an airline stewardess, drawing and painting.

"Mostly gnarled trees," Cotton put in, jarring me because of the infrequency of his words. He guffawed.

"Cotton's gone cubist," Ryan explained.

I couldn't see Cotton as — well, an artist. He'd just got back from Paris, Ryan said, and had even sold some paintings there, out in the street, to American tourists apparently.

"They're whores, that's what they are, whores," he said.

This comment hinted at dark secrets in Cotton's life, passion and bitter loss in the city of love. Was it possible? I glanced at his pink, ingenuous face, and quickly looked away, lest he guffaw and maybe slap his knee.

"So you're really taking the big step this summer?" Ryan asked me.

"Yeah," I said. In the groggy atmosphere of Kelly's, Omaha seemed remote.

I stayed at Rick's till I found an apartment.

That wasn't easy. I finally had to sublet from a bachelor college prof who was going on sabbatical; his little one-room cubicle was in a gigantic apartment complex called the Twin Oaks, right across from the University of Kansas City and near the Plaza. Small but nicely furnished, with abstract prints on the walls, bronze statuettes, Danish Modern furniture, a Japanese screen, and a collection of records and books by guys like Proust and Joyce.

"I just know you'll take good care of them," said the prof, causing Ryan to squint.

My only misgiving was the one-room deal, the two Danish Modern couches with removable backs so you could sleep on them. The marriage beds! But I moved in and was ready to start work. The first day I drove with great care, awed by my every movement, past the Volker fountain, past the Nelson Gallery and Art Institute, down Gillham Road to the huge, square, cream-colored building, to park on the roof beside the eighth floor where it was wedged into a hill. I sought out Bob MacIntyre, smiling, red-faced, bald-headed director of Contemporary Cards.

I had come to work without a tie; what the hell does an artist need with a tie? But Mr. MacIntyre, smiling the while, explained that Mr. Hall expected all the employees to "look sharp." He seemed apologetic. I was sent down to the company shop to buy a tie.

Let me plunge immediately into the situation. The Contemporary department, surprisingly small I thought, was hidden behind the ad department on the ninth floor. At first I was turned on by all the media available, colored paper, lace and gold leaf, bristol board of any ply, sable brushes, all kinds of ink and paint-even old *London Illustrated Gazettes*, with busy engravings which the artists often cut out to give an antique look to a Contemporary Card. I went to work with gusto. Actually, I'd been hired as a writer, but Mr. MacIntyre had told me I could design, too — "if you want to," he'd added, without enthusiasm.

So I made scores of designs, my own originals, and neatly covered them with clear acetate, the way I'd seen the other artists doing it. You put them on racks and they were voted on by the artists, the writers, and people from "media research," whatever that is. All my designs were voted down.

The other artists and writers were nice to me, but I sensed a coldness. They played silly jokes on each other but I felt left out. In my heart of hearts, I was sure they'd heard how I'd been hired, a bit of nepotism. None seemed wild about my work. I still had *Mad*-magazine tendencies, drawing hairy and wart-nosed little figures that I thought were funny. But it wouldn't do; MacIntyre insisted on "cuteness." Morbid humor, beloved of the *Showme* staff, was out here.

There was more to greeting-card design than the drawing of grotesque little figures. You had to know how to juxtapose colors, how to use Zip-a-tone lettering, how to add decorative flourishes. MacIntyre was crazy for "cleanness." And the favorite expression of the artist who sat in the glassed-in cubicle behind me was, "That's *tacky*."

Whatever talent I had seemed to be obscured by these professionals. But I was eager to learn. I'd watch them carefully, ask questions which seemed to amuse them, but only slightly. For creators of humorous cards, they seemed somewhat devoid of humor, except when they were playing jokes on each other or satirizing MacIntyre. I became aware of rivalries, bitterness.

Several were frustrated fashion designers. Most dreamed of going to New York. They complained about drawing "neuters," those cute little Nebbish figures you see on studio cards, made sexless so either men or women can buy them.

But there was a certain freedom there.

MacIntyre didn't watch us, and we almost never saw Mr. Hall, who hovered over the other departments. We could do a lot of what we wanted, play records, have Mexican jumping-bean races, even go off on little jaunts around town. We usually ate at the Crown Room, right in the building, but sometimes we'd go out and stay hours. One day we all went to the Mardi Gras, a jazz joint on 16th and Vine, where one of the staff artists had just completed a mural. He was very good.

Drinking a martini and gazing at the brilliant mardi gras scene, l thought about going back to school, to the Art Institute or somewhere, to make up for the Lost Time of Journalism School.

I'd been at Hallmark about a month when it was time to get married. I took two days off for a long weekend in Omaha and, drunk most of the time, managed to get the job done.

"We can't bring all that back with us," I told my bride, referring to the wedding gifts.

"But I need some good china."

"All you think about is material things," I raged.

But I loved her, she seemed new again. I brought my bride and a carload of material things back to K.C.

We were mostly together. K.C. was the big city, with lots of things to do, Mexican food at Margarita's on the Plaza, drinks at Milton's on 33rd and Main, live jazz at the Mardi Gras, Bettye Miller and Milt Abel cutting up at the Horseshoe Lounge. Sometimes Ryan and his airline stewardess were with us. They came over for dinner in our hot, sticky, but very arty apartment.

We sat outside and watched the stars. Sometimes we went to art shows where Ryan's work was displayed; he was indeed specializing in gnarled trees, watercolor landscapes, bright and shimmery but somewhat tacky.

At the Red Barn playhouse, where we saw *The Importance of Being Earnest*, the walls were filled with Ryans, like a good page in a stamp album. And I sometimes took long walks, by myself, down the abandoned railroad tracks that ran south from behind the Twin Oaks.

I was also loning it at work. The others could waste time with practical jokes and jumping-bean races; I would take off in the afternoon and drive down to the Nelson Art Gallery. Sometimes I would go to just one room, as often as not the one with oriental sculpture, Chinese or Japanese, I forget which. It was very hushed in there; the irony I was tired of froze in the presence of the bodhisattvas, the Kwan Yin figures of painted wood. There was little light. The far wall was a Buddhist wall painting of some kind, huge, the original reconstructed here in rectangular blocks. In the midst of the faded reds and greens sat Buddah, serene, contemplative. Having been reading Suzuki and Kerouac, I considered myself a Buddhist. I'd stand there all solemn, worshipping God or Art or my own melancholy.

But it was fun, too, being young and in love in K.C. If the cabin cruiser was drifting away to Avalon, there was something else rising up on the horizon, something serious, sort of scary. But only when you were alone. The main thing, when you were with others, was the fun you had. I had never before been so aware of fun.

Ryan was telling me about Cotton's new adventures. Somewhere or other he'd made the acquaintance of an old lady, a dowager, a widow with money who considered herself a patroness of the arts. She had purchased several acres of dense woodland which she dreamed of making into a park. She was delighted to meet Cotton, who had been to Europe, and wondered if he'd be interested in doing some sculpture on the indigenous rock that abounded there. You know, satyrs and nymphs and other classical subjects.

Eventually she would clear some trees, cultivate a sward and flower garden, build fountains and stone benches and winding paths, where dreamers could lose themselves in the beauty of nature improved. Sure, Cotton would be interested.

So she hired him, buying his tools and paying him a small weekly wage. The tools he purchased were an ordinary ballpeen hammer and a chisel. Cotton had never done any stone sculpture, a fact he didn't bother mentioning to the dowager, but there was no time like the present to try.

One fine Saturday we set out for the old lady's park. My wife and the stewardess had prepared a picnic. The city fell behind us, Ryan was telling stories from a Lenny Bruce record, and my wife sat very close to me as I drove. We bumped over a dirt road, came to a wide space in it, and Ryan told me to stop.

"This is it," he said. "This?"

It looked like any wooded area in Missouri, mostly scrub oak, a damp, unpleasant odor hanging over everything. It was all very rank, very prickly looking, nature unimproved, fit for squirrels and children but hardly old ladies. There were vines to swing on. I half expected to look up and see a tree house.

"Listen," said Ryan.

I thought I could hear a woodpecker tapping. "That's Cotton," Ryan grinned.

We made our way along a path he found behind some milkweed, I with the picnic basket, dodging limbs and bramble bushes.

"Ugh," said my wife, rubbing her face. "Whatsamatter, honey?" I asked.

"Cobwebs."

"Look," Ryan stopped and pointed.

I would have missed it. There were rocks of various sizes along the path, mostly limestone, but this one had apparently been chipped at by a human being. It looked slightly like a Coke bottle.

"What is it?" asked Ryan's girl.

"Pan playing his pipes," he said.

We went on, the tapping getting louder. We saw more rocks that had been chipped at, all of them resembling nothing so much as rocks that had been chipped at. Finally, we got to a clearing, thick with grass and purple flowers. Here there were more rocks; all of them over two feet high had been attacked with the chisel. None was very large. Several were vaguely anthropomorphic, but you could see where an arm had been accidently knocked off, where the attempt to make a crotch had split an entire rock.

"See, he doesn't know anything about the grain," said Ryan, grinning. "Just starts chipping away with the hammer and chisel. He's got a thing about satyrs. He won't give up till he makes a good one."

Poor Cotton. What would the old lady say when she saw his work, some of which — unintentionally, I'm sure — resembled phalluses?

Grasshoppers zipped out of our way as we swished through the grass to a muddy little creek, shaded by sycamores. Everyone dropped whatever he was carrying.

"Hey, let's have a beer," I said.

"Yeah," said Ryan, opening the cooler. "You guys spread the blankets and take it easy. I'm gonna take one to Cotton."

Rick set out in the direction of the tapping.

Meanwhile, we spread the blankets, opened beers, and reclined in the daze of nature unimproved, except for the ruins of Cotton's sculpture, which you couldn't even see from here for the thick grass.

I lay on my back, half raised on my elbows, gazing at the woods across the creek. Ryan appeared like Apollo amidst the foliage.

"How," he said, raising his right hand. "White devil speak with forked tongue."

He sprinted across the clearing, jumped the creek, scrambled up the little embankment, and collapsed beside his stewardess, whose slacks he unzipped.

"Rick," she said, slapping his hand away.

"How's Michelangelo?" I asked.

"Not bad, but he's giving up on satyrs. He's doing a big head now, Zeus or somebody."

"Is he coming over?"

"Not just yet. Don't worry, as soon as he chips off the nose he'll give up for the day."

So we brought out the lunch, the fried chicken potato salad baked beans celery stalks and radishes. We put away beer and food, slapped at the bugs, tickled our ladies, loafed in the shade of the sycamores. Lazily, Ryan tossed stones in the creek. It was fun, it was fun being there in the shade on the blankets on the grass, the scene was for now forever, it was Manet's *Le Dejeuner sur l'herbe* (though both girls were dressed) — or perhaps, considering the speckled patterns of leaves and their shadows, the yellow-greens and violets, something more elusive, more impressionistic, as if the girls should be in long dresses with bustles and parasols, the men in straw hats and mustaches and white shirts, as the sunlight changed continuously on the grass and, somewhere, someone was tap-tapping, just at the edge of the daydream.

Biography and Photographs

William Joseph Zander was born on April 28, 1938, in Tulsa, Oklahoma to Edmund Leonard Zander and Florence Zimmerman Zander. He was raised in Omaha, Nebraska and attended colleges in Arizona, Missouri, and Iowa. He was a graduate of the Missouri School of Journalism at the University of Missouri in Columbia. He was a graduate of the Missouri School of Journalism at the University of Missouri in Columbia, where he received a master's degree in English. He attended the Iowa Writer's Workshop.

Bill was a Professor Emeritus of English and Journalism at the Florham Campus of Fairleigh Dickinson University in New Jersey, having taught there for over four decades before his retirement. He was a founding faculty member of the MFA in Creative Writing Program.

He was a widely published poet and poetry editor of several literary magazines. He was the author of two collections of poetry, *Distances* and *Gone Haywire*, and a chapbook, *Winter Trees*. Bill was a regular reader at the First Tuesday meetings of the literary group, the Writers' Roundtable in Newton, NJ.

He served on the board of the Crandon Lakes Property Owners' Association for several seasons. A life-long environmentalist, he was an expert fly-tier and fly fisherman and published articles on a variety of outdoor and environmental subjects for many periodicals.

He was devoted to human rights issues and spent many years using his bi-lingual abilities to write letters in support of unjustly imprisoned journalists and other victims of human-rights violations for Amnesty International.

He was a member of Christ Episcopal Church in Newton and served as a lector, usher, and member of the Altar Guild. He regularly attended Bible Study and helped in a number of outreach programs.

Bill died on April 3, 2019. He is survived by his wife, the former Alexandria Halloran Hughes; a step-son, Joshua Hughes of Long Valley, NJ; two sons, Gabriel Zander of Hampton Twp. and Adlai Zander of Broadalbin, NY; four grandchildren—Sebastien Hughes, Astrid Hughes, Simon Florio, and Tillulah Zander; a brother, James Zander of Bellingham, WA; and several nieces and nephews. He was predeceased by his brother Michael Zander

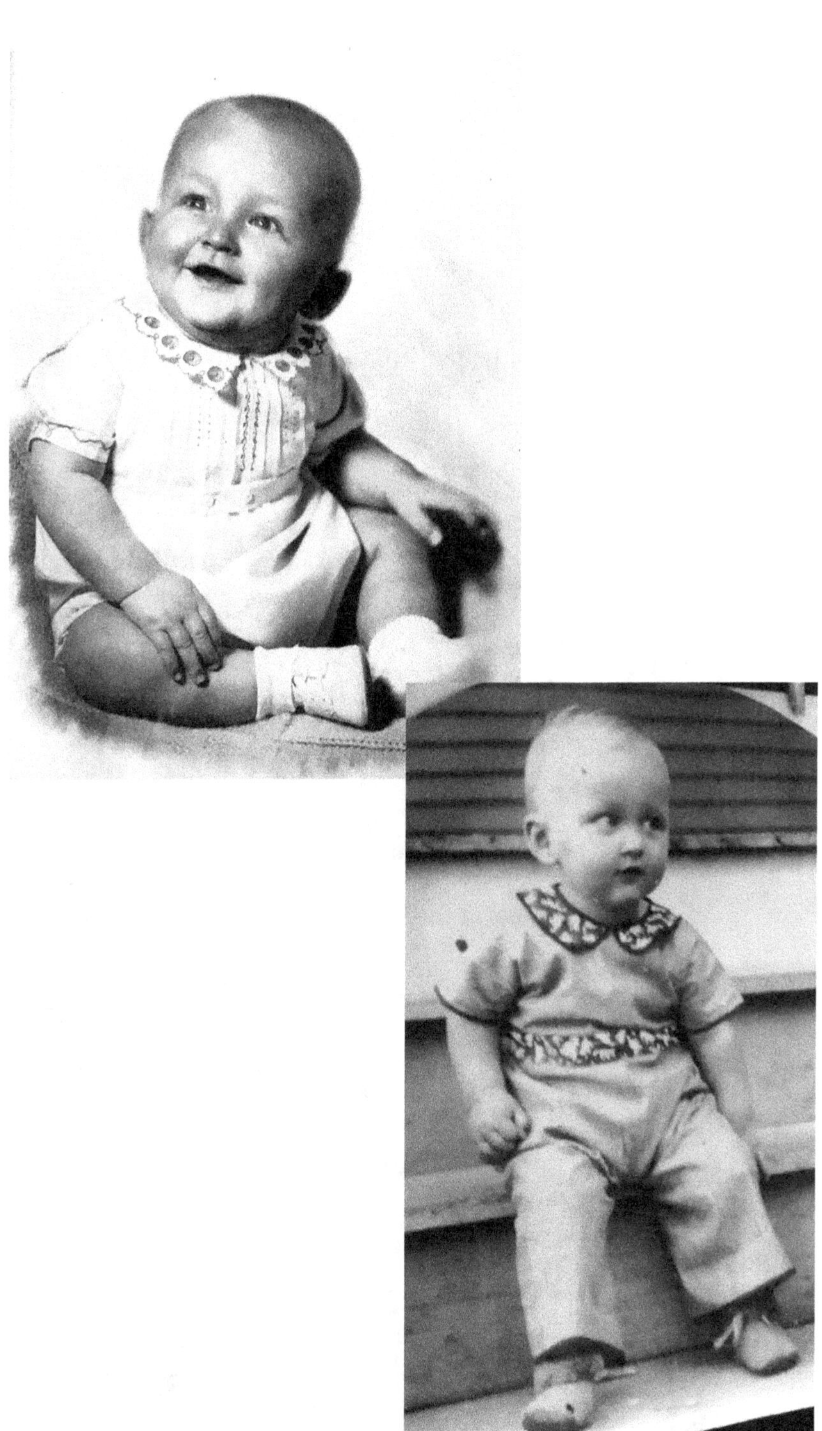

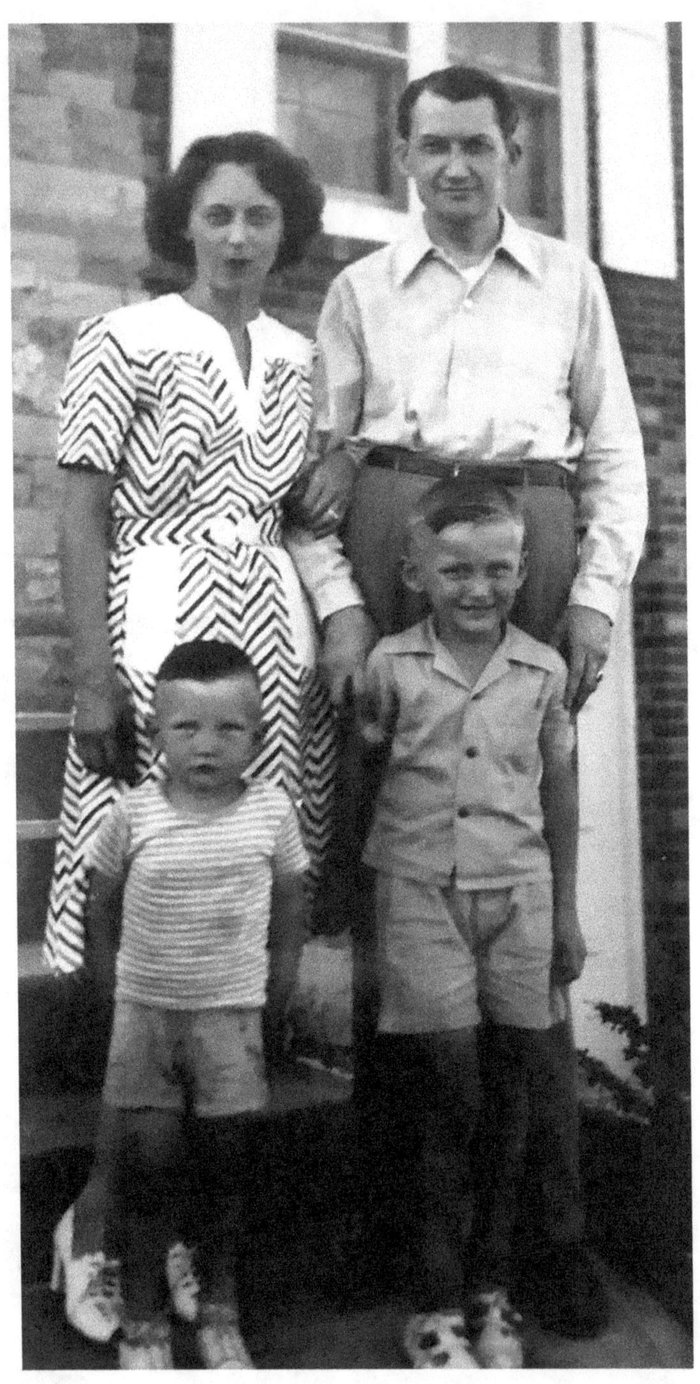

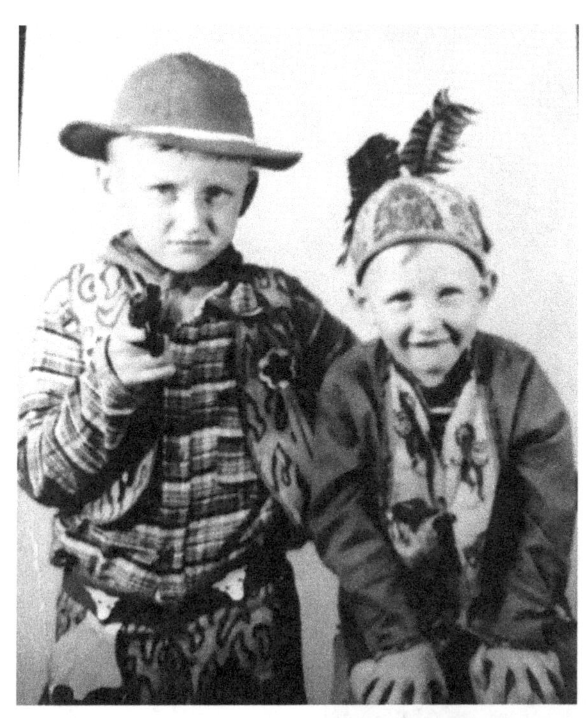

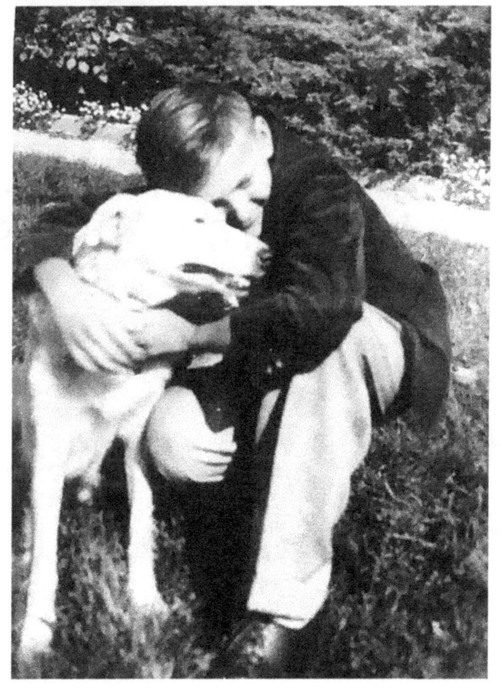

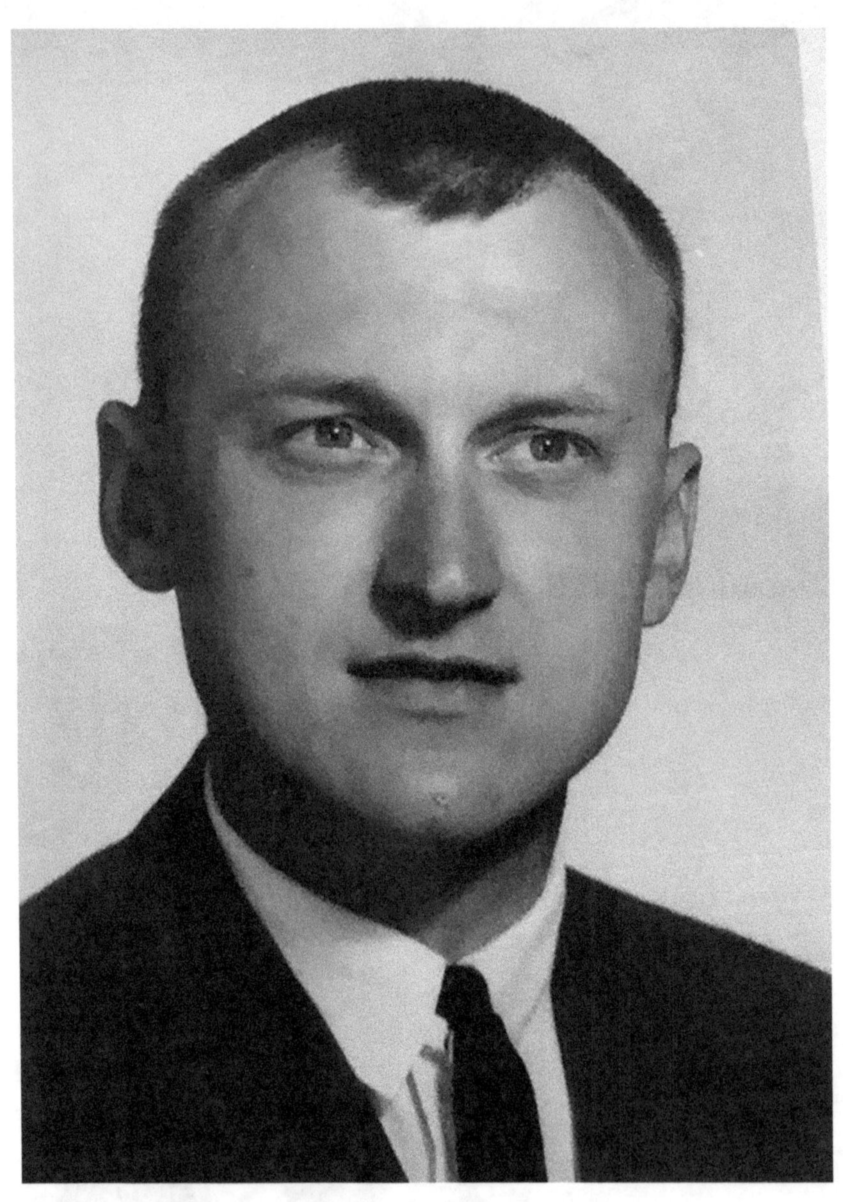

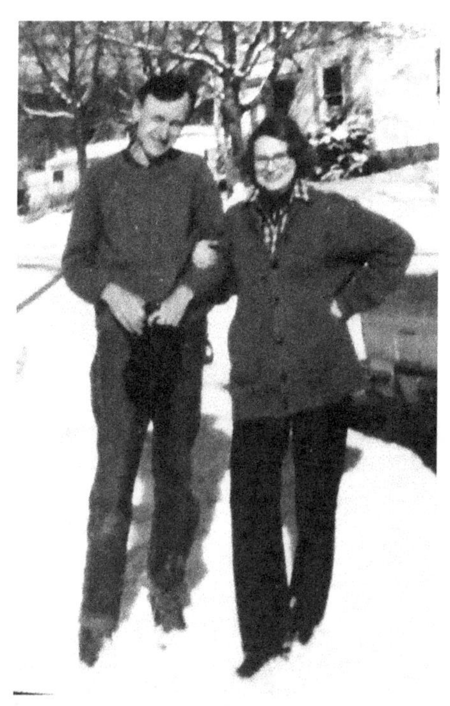

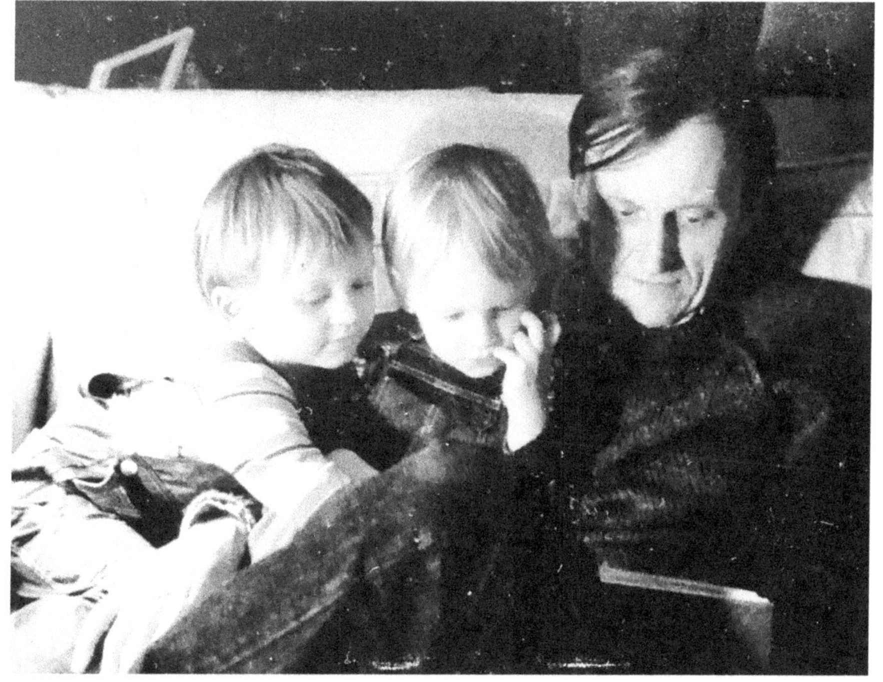

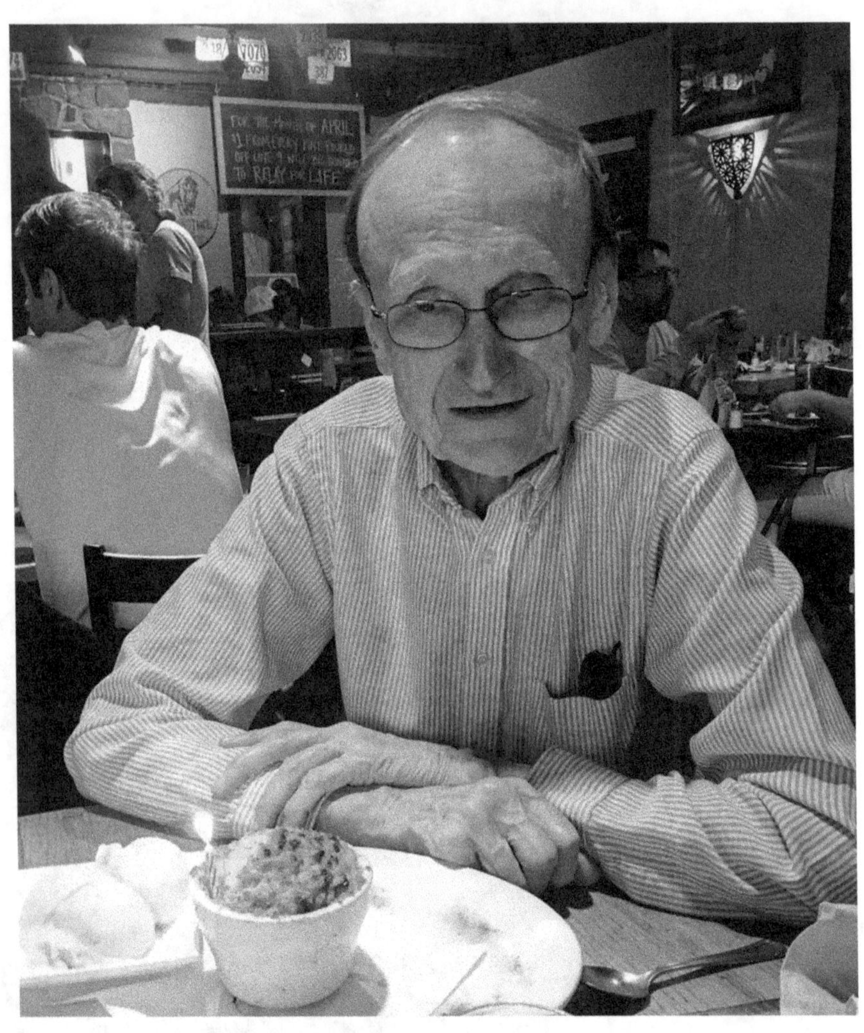

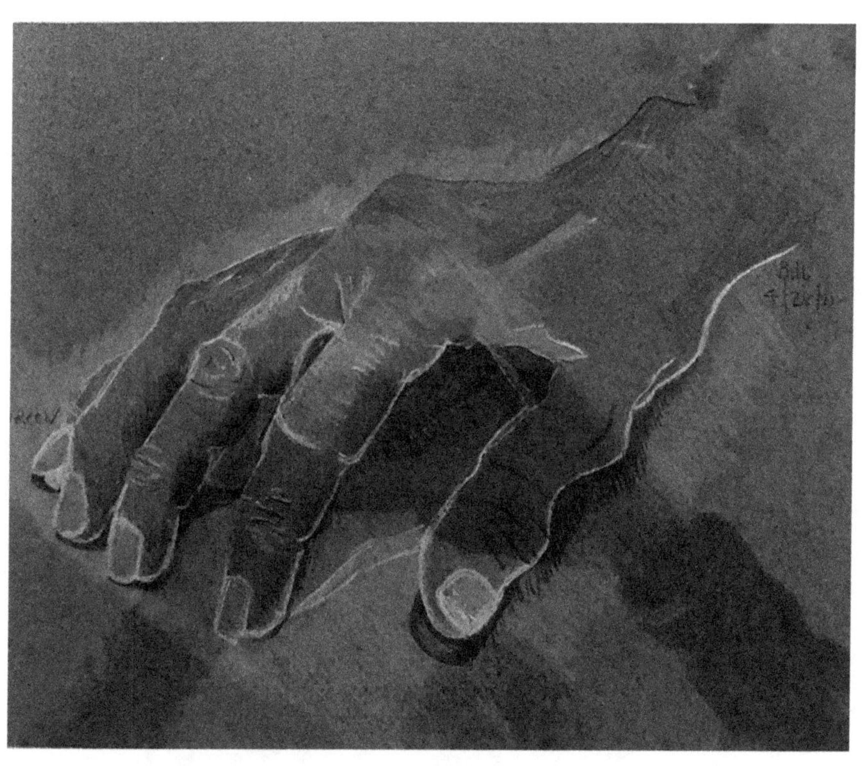

Bill Zander hand by Maureen Slamer

Memories

Alex Zander

Part I of the Bill's Memorial Sermon
Christ Church, Newton NJ
April 27, 2019

One morning I stood next to Bill Zander as this Gospel that you just heard was read. The priest had no more than intoned the phrase, "In the beginning was the Word" when Bill snapped to attention and said, "YES!" in a voice loud enough to be heard in the far corners of the church.

I later suggested that a simple "Amen, brother" might have been appropriate — even in that serene, reserved, very Episcopalian setting. But, you see, it wasn't Bill Zander, wannabe Baptist, who reacted so viscerally to the gospel of John. It was Bill Zander, the poet. The craftsman who saw words the way environmentalists see a mountain or a stream: as gifts from God; things to be cherished and protected, nurtured and tended, eased — or teased — into their full potential. It was Bill, the poet, the steward of words, with whom that phrase resonated.

Over the years his reaction to this rather astonishing account of creation was always the same, an almost child-like act of affirmation. In a sense, it was a mutual affirmation, Bill recognizing and embracing that text as his own and that text recognizing and embracing Bill as its own.

For Bill the designation, poet, came with a price. It demanded dedication and a reverence for words and the willingness to work hard at the craft of putting them together. Writing poetry also demanded a willingness to stare into the face of things too difficult for many people to address, much less transform into works of art. "Seeing the bones beneath the skin" was his favorite way of putting it. And the end result? Well, it was a way of communicating things that seemed impossible to communicate (the "shock of recognition" — another phrase he loved dearly), that something might resonate with someone as that text of John resonated with him.

Over the past fifteen or so years I watched Bill fall in love. I think I was in a pretty good position to know what that looked like — I'd seen it before . . . Wherever you are in this space today, you are in the midst of the object of his affection. He fell in love with Christ Church, with the congregation here — his second family. He fell in love with the intelligence, good humor and spiritual direction of our rector, Robert. He fell in love with the beauty and the discipline of the worship services. He fell in love with the dignity accredited every human being who walked through the doors. But most of all he fell head over heels in love with Jesus — the Word incarnate, the Word made flesh, the Word who dwelt among us — and used words.

Jesus means many different things to many different people. There are those for whom the sacrifice of Jesus is the focus of their relationship with him, those for whom the promise of Easter, the Resurrection, is their focus, those for whom Jesus provides comfort when there is no other comfort to be found . . . But for Bill, his relationship with Jesus was one of pure delight. You could see it in his regular attendance at Bible study and the preparations and after-study that he indulged himself in.

Bill Zander, the lover and manipulator of words, who could take a tired, shop-worn cliché and flip it into a breath-taking image that would (sorry, Bill) "knock your socks off" couldn't help but be drawn to the Jesus with whom he felt a writer's kinship.

He loved reading the Gospels, particularly the parables. He loved the way Jesus turns the common wisdom on its ear. He loved the way Jesus uses rhetorical questions that backfire. For example, take the parable of the good shepherd. Just as you're about to agree that of course the shepherd should go after one lousy sheep, you realize that ninety-nine are left in jeopardy of being eaten by wolves and you rethink the common wisdom. It's a lunatic move. Suddenly Jesus has pulled the rug out from under you and made you see that the Kingdom of Heaven is ridiculous by our standards of justice and fairness. God doesn't play by our rules. And Jesus says, "Gotcha!"

Bill loved these sly turns. He saw Jesus as a trickster. One whose words could be read and re-read with new meanings and layers of meanings unfolding every time — the Word that can't be nailed down, not even to a cross.

Many of us have notions of what we would hope for our loved ones who have died. My hope for Bill is that his is an eternity of delight. A face-to-face encounter with the Word unfolding in new configurations, moment by moment, never-ending, fresh forever. The Word that never becomes a cliché.

The Reverend Canon Robert Griner

Part II of the Bill's Memorial Sermon
Christ Church, Newton NJ
April 27, 2019

And the Word became flesh and dwelt among us.

Famous last words. Bill was a man of words. And he had a few famous last words, the ones I heard. We've got some history, 15 years. So I was listening, for the words, as he approached the end. Famous last words. He told me he loved me. And not some throwaway line, but looking up at me with those beautiful blue eyes, he said it like he meant it and I think he did.

His actual Famous last words to me, the very last words, were closer to the end; as I approached his bed he was slipping in and out of consciousness. Ever the attentive and sensitive priest, I consulted the priest manual in my mind, which functions kind of like a marriage manual. Helpful, but clunky and mechanical at times. Step # 1 Ascertain patient's orientation. Not orientation as it is commonly used nowadays, that might have been distracting to the family, but, rather, is the church member oriented to place. time, and person? Best practices. Advanced priestcraft I'm letting you in on.

So, I said, Bill, do you know who I am? I had better sense than to ask a poet, Bill do you know who you are? I wouldn't be able to stand the musings, the patter, on and on and on.

He answered, without hesitation, You are Don Edwards. Now I would later discover that Don Edwards was a mythical character in the Zander family lexicon, who had not been conjured up for years. Don Edwards was, as Alex explained, a man who had never had an original idea in his whole life, a man who buys a brown car, an everyman, another bozo on the bus.

Thanks Bill. No, I mean it, thanks Bill. The first half of my life

I dedicated myself to becoming a cut above, a rare breed, someone rather special, the kind of person Bill Zander couldn't abide. The second half of my life I've given it a good run at being ordinary, common, just like everyone else. Don Edwards. I took this as Bill's great revelation at the end, Famous Last Words: I'm just a dude dying. Being assisted by a rather unremarkable priest. Wonderful Liberty! Free at last. Merging with his Savior

In Greek there are two ways to say flesh or body. One is soma, the other sarx. Now soma is the flesh of youth, fecundity and lithesome promise. Athletic Greek statues are soma all the way.

Sarx, on the other hand, always refers to the human body pejoratively. To have sarx is an unfavorable thing. Our sarx gets sick, it smells, it grows old, it dies.

This is the word we find in the first Chapter of John, sarx not soma. The word of God became flesh sarx. God in hot pursuit of our broken, creaky body. The incarnation of Jesus was into the stinky, sweaty unattractive sarx world. Bill Zander was sarx kinda guy all the way. He wrote sarx poetry. He had a sarx body. The guy was skin and bones all his life. You would never have mistaken him for Charles Atlas. You could tell by his body that it was his mind that Alex fell in love with. But it was his sarx she lovingly washed when he had died.

Mortal, can these bones live? The Lord asks Ezekiel. Bill read this prophecy for a decade in the dark at our most sarx service of the year, the Easter Vigil. Can these bones live? I suppose so, Bill would answer. O my people, (speaking for God). I will put my spirit within you, and you shall live

Did you ever see Bill in his classic pose? Arms wrapped around himself. For years, I thought, what is he doing? Is he cold? Nervous? What is that? I think he was just trying to hold it all in, lest it just gush out on the floor in front of everyone. What he felt for the whole world. How undone he was by so much senseless suffering.

In 1975 when Francisco Franco died, the brutal dictator of Spain, famous for killing thousands of artists and poets, there was widespread celebration throughout the lefty world. When the word spread to young Alex and Bill and their hip, artsy friends there was wild jubilation except for one. Who was silent, out of sync with the others.

Alex said, Bill you're not happy? Bill answered simply, I don't think I could ever celebrate the death of another human being.

This one is for me. Jesus-y to the bone.

To all that Bill held in his guts, in his splachna, barely containing it, all the sin of the world, God's response is the Body of Christ. It was Bill's answer. The sarx of Christ ascended into heaven, Michelangelo got it right when he depicted Jesus reigning in heaven, his body still pierced with sword, his palm still penetrated. The Body of Christ, the sacrament, the broken chunks we pass out that touch us in our brokenness. The Body of Christ, the Church, the sarx of Christ, very flawed but still able to breathe life into dead bones.

The Body of Christ.
Nothing Special. Everything.

Gabe Zander

Anyone who knew Bill Zander on a personal level will certainly remember his iron clad beliefs about all that which is good and right, but with a rather easy-going approach to how to go about putting said beliefs into practice.

To me, this system of inner-reconciliation can be summed up with one little adage he used to say to us when we were kids: "Well, don't make yourself SICK ..." (note the accenting denoted by the punctuation and capitalization there; more on that in a minute).

The funny thing about this seemingly profound-locked-into-the-simple advice is that he never meant it as such, even amidst all the things he did mean that way ("De gustabus non disputandumest," "Stand up for what you believe in," my brother's aforementioned "Go to the bathroom when you have to," etc.). No, he only ever said it at mealtime, when one of us labored to finish everything on an overly full plate, and he could see whichever child it was beginning to eat slowly, and what food we could bear to put in our mouths about ready to jump back out onto said plate.

Every occasion I remember him saying that, he was "off the-clock" as a wordsmith; it wasn't coming from William Zander the poet, or Professor William Zander lecturing to a class of bright-eyed college students, or *New Jersey Herald* staff writer William Zander writing a profound opinion piece that might alter public attitudes about this that or the other issue and thereby save our fragile planet or whatever, or even our dear father sitting us down each on one knee giving us a life lesson with the intention of "helping us out down the road."

Nah, it was just my dad saying what came to mind on one particular occasion that repeated itself here and there, and specific to that detail of our lives whenever it arose. Didn't take an English Professor or published poet to spit that one out. He could have been a sewer worker, a street sweeper, or even Donald Trump and still come up with it.

Any dad, noticing his son stuffing his face when obviously full or at least getting there: "Well, don't make yourself SICK . . ."

He thought nothing of it and neither did I. Well, I didn't at the time anyway, and I'm pretty sure he went the rest of his life having just forgotten about it.

But later I began to realize that pretty much everything he believed in, when it came to balancing a commitment to what we hold dear with simple self-care, could be summed up in that little package: "Well, don't make yourself SICK . . ."

In the same way we have to eat, we need to do things with ourselves, and just like how we need to eat actual nourishment rather than eating ice cream all day we have to act on things that give our lives meaning ("Here's your dinner"), but at the same time when we get overloaded with worry about said things-from-which-we-draw-meaning, things completely unravel and they all-come to naught: "Well, don't make yourself SICK . . ."

Oh right, the accenting. The punctuation and capitalization I've been using are about as close as I could get to Dad's voice in print; you'll notice how it seems to leave the book open. Whereas a simple "Don't make yourself sick (period)" would denote final-ity, as if to say "Stop eating," the way Dad said it left it up to the listener.

"Sure, finish all that's on your plate if you absolutely must, but I'm just saying you won't lose face if you don't; in fact, it's silly to force yourself. Either way the choice is yours, but I'm giving you a preview of what might happen if you push it too hard."

Dad was a lifelong environmentalist; so he recycled, contrib-uted to conservation groups, and offset his consumerism by eating some of the fish he caught and wild mushrooms he found in the field; but knew his limits when it came to adopting a strict vegan diet or blowing up an animal testing lab in a carefully orchestrated midnight covert operation.

Dad was a supporter of the civil rights movement, so he re-frained from shopping or eating at "No Colored" business in his hometown of Omaha or where he went to college in Missouri, and never hid his stance on the matter no matter how many friends it could lose somebody in the 1950's Midwest or Midsouth; south; but I don't recall any stories of him climbing to the roof of a building overlooking a Klan rally with a clear line of sight for the scope on his .30-06 rifle (though I wasn't around for his younger days, so if anyone wants to correct me on that . . .).

Dad was tough, there's no question, though that might not be the first word that comes to mind in describing him. He was generally of a calm and/or polite demeanor in talking to strangers, rarely at odds with friends or family, and it can't be repeated that he was anything but overbearing as a father. No, he pushed himself, and sometimes even us, in different ways.

A passionate woodsman, he preferred to go off the trails and bushwack, often challenging me to follow when, as a younger child, my apiphobia (that is, a fear of stinging insects) made me apprehensive about accompanying him into the denser thickets for fear I might stumble into a nest of paper wasps, and of course I had to end up sucking it up and following along.

At 65, before he'd retired from teaching, he was T-boned out of the backseat of a car Mom was driving and dashed his head straight through the window and out onto concrete and, while initially knocked clean out, was going over his lesson plans for the following fall within a week.

The last time we went hiking, about a month after he'd turned 80, we covered 6 miles with about a thousand foot, repeatedly alternating variance in elevation, and only brought a couple granola bars; he took a fall into some of those trademark jagged Kitatinny mountain rocks and my first thought was we'd need a medivac. He just asked me for a hand up and after a brief rest, finished wearing out both me and my 23-year-old ladyfriend who had joined us.

When his physical fitness finally wore down to the point of little or no "adventures," he kept up bringing in firewood, washing the dishes, whatever he felt needed done at any given time.

And when his health finally got to the point that his life could only be prolonged by revolving his life around doctors' visits, when his activities were pretty much whittled down to watching TV and seeing how much food he could stomach at whatever given time, he showed his brazenness in the face of the primal human fear of death and simply said "nope!" — although with perhaps a few more expletives than would be appropriate here.

He knew he had a full plate, but took his time finishing his dinner. Whenever he began to "make himself sick," he'd politely excuse himself from the table.

So to anyone who wishes to "honor" Bill Zander (whatever the hell that means, and as if he ever cared or would care now about such things), I say hold fast to what is right, try to do everything you feel inclined to, but don't lose your head over it.

In a nutshell, don't make yourself sick. This time with a period.

Adlai Zander

Bill Zander was my father, teacher & mentor. I've never known a man more stalwart and consistent in character than he was, absolutely unshakeable in his adherence to what he felt to be true. In spite of this, he never forced or imposed his values on anyone, even his children. His approach to parenting was devoid of any "because I said so" dogma. Humility was perhaps the most important virtue to him. I like to think he took Ben Franklin's ironically simple approach — be more like Socrates and Jesus. And like these two iconic historic/literary characters, my father would express his feelings and opinions freely and often adamantly. But as all good teachers do, he admitted and acknowledged wherein he fell short of empirical knowledge or experience. Though he was a talented & enthusiastic lecturer, he didn't spend much time at home giving preachy, life-lesson type speeches. In regards to his obligatory responsibility to give "fatherly advice," he would almost universally invoke his sacred adage — "go to the bathroom when you have to," in a mocking tone of authority. It seemed like a joke when I was young, but as life progressed, I saw how important and very deep this message could be. I thought about it many times when I was trapped by my circumstances in a situation that didn't allow for micturation (his personal favorite term for it). New Jersey rush-hour interstate commuting gives one much time to chew on such gristle of wisdom. It was certainly one thing I saw him take extremely literally right up till his dying day. It might seem like a petty rule, but taking care of the little things that are entirely your responsibility and well within your means to control, can make all the difference in your ability to accomplish anything, great or small. Just think about how much harder anything in life can be when you really just need to pee? After all, it's hard to be a good person if you don't take care of yourself. Sure, he also taught me to love and respect others, never to judge by appearance alone, not to strive for material gain over personal integrity, to be a faithful witness, and perhaps most of all, to appreciate what we have been given as conscious participants in an infinitely complex and rewarding universe of experience. These lessons were mostly taught by example. Very few were as inscribed in stone as — "go to the bathroom when you have to." So do please heed Bill Zander's words, and if you haven't already, tell your children.

Joshua Hughes

Should I have thought: "Was I abducted?"
Heck, half of all kidnappings occur by family members and most
frequently under the age of 6. The FBI says so.

I was 6.
Riding in an undistinguished station wagon, on the lam from NJ
to some western parts unknown.
Mom was there. Clearly guilty.
And this curious, tall, dark-haired stranger.

Consider this:
I was perhaps too naïve to know all the initiation rites of gang
membership, but I recall one summer morning on the dock of
a Minnesota lake. I clearly remember having a barbed fishing
hook fully pierce my ear. "Oh, sure kid! You did it yourself while
casting" I can hear them say, but I ask you: Who was the expert
angler? Who would know how to weight a lure "just right" to
ensure it would take the proper trajectory to affix itself to me?
Who would be there in a moment's notice to snip off the barb
and "destroy the evidence"? I would come to learn more about
this mysterious man.

We could have lived out our days in Minnesota, never visiting
the same lake twice, but we pushed on toward California: The
sanctuary state. There we met up with "The Zanders". At the
time, the ringleader may have been Ed, but I'm pretty sure the
one they called "Bill" had designs of his own. (AH! He has a
name!) Bill was proving himself to be independent AND loyal
to the cause. A casual reader would surely know my fate was
sealed.

Here's some anecdotal insight into how Bill indoctrinated me:
• For an outsider, he treated me with a surprising amount of respect and love
• He provided food, shelter, and education, building a cycle of dependency
• I was taught a surprising number of life skills
• After my undergraduate education, I may have been seen as a flight risk and was brought back into the fold by attending the very same university where Bill taught.

He had me.

So, reader beware. I believe I can truthfully answer my original question: I was fully abducted and raised in the "Bill Zander Cult of Parenting."

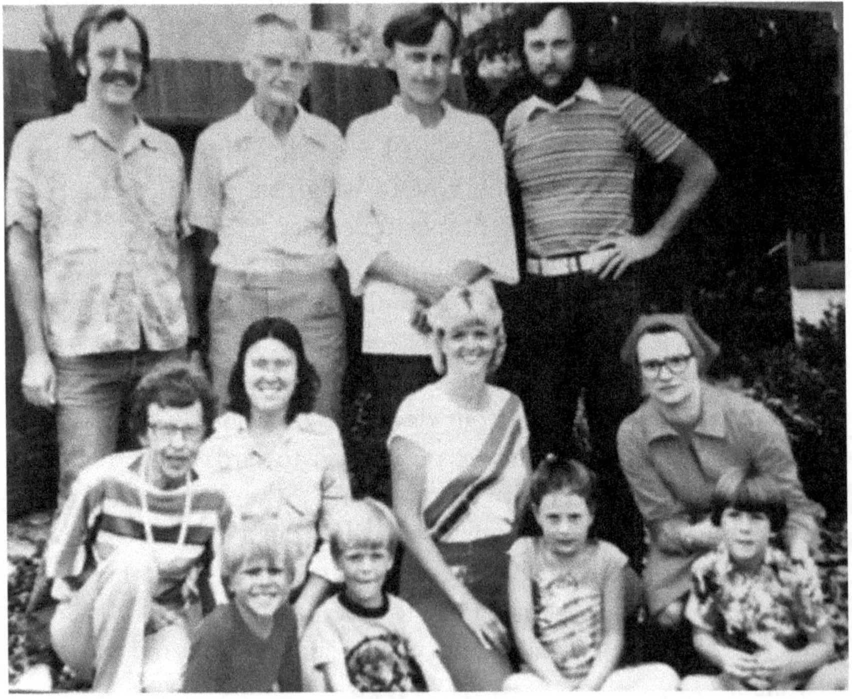

Back row: Mike, Ed, Bill, and Jim Zander; middle row: Florence, Sharon, Nanci, and Alex Zander; bottom row: Joshua Hughes and Scott, Jennifer, and Ian Zander

Jim Zander

Most people know that Bill played the guitar and sang. But most people don't know that Bill appeared on the Johnny Carson show. That's right. But it was not the *Tonight Show*. In the early 50's, Johnny had an afternoon show on WOW-TV in Omaha, Nebraska. When Bill was about 13, he was invited to pick and sing the hit country & western song, "Don't Let the Stars Get in Your Eyes" on Johnny's show. Johnny went on to become a national TV icon. Bill never made it to Nashville.

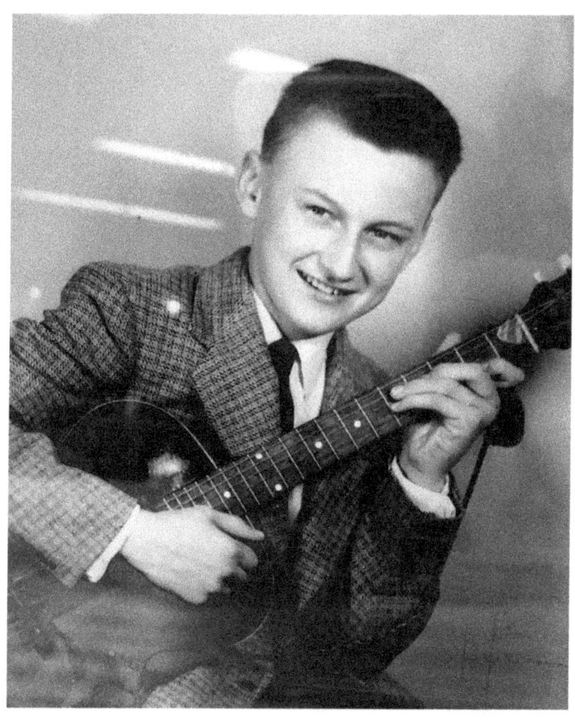

*

Bill and I attended Benson High School in Omaha. The Benson Bunnies! Bill was a senior and I was a freshman. Bill was very popular, a good student, but had some "disagreements" with some of the teachers and staff. One of Bill's good friends wrote in my yearbook: "If you work hard you can clear up the name of ZANDER at Benson. I don't think you'll do it though".

*

When Bill would threaten to run away from home, Dad would offer him $500 to do it. Bill never took him up on it.

Walter Cummins

Bill Zander had been an ongoing friend and presence in my life since 1961 — almost sixty years ago — when he arrived to take a technical writing instructors' desk in the Engineering Building at the University of Iowa, a tall, very thin young man with a standup crew cut. Since that day our lives intertwined, across three states and on one Balearic island.

When Alex, Bill's wife, called the afternoon of April 3, 2019, to tell me that he had died very peacefully — just stopped breathing, expired, I thought I would feel relieved. He had been in hospice care for more than a week, agitated initially, then just signaling for water to moisten his mouth and lips, in restless unconsciousness. His wife and sons had taken turns sitting by his bedside, sleeping little, alert for the end. Death would be a release for Bill and for them. I hoped for it. The actuality, though — the raw fact of it — hit me with a profound and unexpected grief.

Bill was unique, unlike any other friend I ever had; multiply talented, consistently witty, frequently zany, with a distinct way of speaking that matched the meter of his poetry. When our department chair told him that his popularity as a teacher had attracted a large following of students, Bill emulated his vision of that following: a stiff-kneed, arms stretched, zombie lurching down the hallway.

Bill was also a man of sincere rectitude, a word he liked to use, not for self-congratulation, but because the sound of it pleased him. He was amused when another chair spared him committee assignments in the belief that Bill was too sensitive a poet to be burdened with the mundane. When he did find himself on committees, however, Bill took the responsibility very seriously, just as he did his commitment to students, despite his classroom clowning.

After learning of his death, one former student wrote me, "I had so much fun in his poetry class. I've often thought of him and his fabulous poetry: there was one poem about getting stoned at a young friend's funeral and another about making a room come to order like Hitler." Another student said, "Bill understood the value of exposing students like myself to a wide range of quality writers. He mentored me through my first published chapbook, which he edited, and helped me win thousands of dollars, the ultimate validation at that time for a would-be professional writer."

When asked to teach journalism courses (he had a bachelors in journalism from the University of Missouri before earning his master's in English there), Bill decided to spend the summer working at a local newspaper so he could learn the then-new digital technology so that his students would also be up-to-date. Although, he did disparage his own undergraduate journalism courses, mocking one in particular that did little more than cope, as he would say, with tickertape output.

Bill chose poetry as his artistic outlet. He published in many literary magazines, had two poetry collections, *Distances* and *Gone Haywire and Other Old Sayings,* and one chapbook. But he could have succeeded equally in any number of creative outlets, and if he hadn't become a teacher he might have supported himself with a career at Hallmark cards, his first job after college, where his verbal and visual wit were a perfect match for the company's comic line.

In Iowa City, Bill and his then-wife, Sara Lee, lived in the suburb of Coralville, in the basement flat of a house owned by a medical student with a two-year-old son who constantly played with himself, to his parents' alarm and embarrassment — and to Bill's amusement.

In their Coralville flat, they owned a black and white TV (we had none), where we would, with our then-wives, watch the very limited offerings of 1930s gangster movies that we called "You Sap" movies because of that term's frequent use in dialogue.

They shared that flat with an orange tomcat called Philip (really Philly Joe Jones), who sought out fierce confrontations with rats, returning home with bites and torn ears, requiring frequent visits to vets. Bill liked to name things. His car at the time was a ponderous, wallowing, pale green DeSoto that he dubbed Henry

James. Later, when he taught creative writing, he told his students to call the course Otto, influenced by John Lennon answering "George" when asked what he called his haircut. A Beatles' fan, Bill had been far ahead of his time, publishing an essay on the genius of the Beatles a year ahead of Richard Poirier's much more influential article in *The Partisan Review.*

Beyond studying poetry at Iowa with Don Justice and fiction with Verlin Cassill, Bill played the guitar and wrote songs (my favorite of his lyrics comes from "When It's Summertime in Maine"—"When the bougainvillea blooms / we will look for furnished rooms"). He also sketched very well and once gave me a book of his drawings that included the elaborate carved-framed Victorian mirror behind the bar at Donnelly's, an occasional Iowa City alternative to the writers' hangout, Kenny's. Bill possessed an encyclopedic knowledge of jazz. Who else could refer to the obscure clarinetist Alcide "Yellow" Nunez in a work of fiction — as if the reader should know who that was?

Aside from writing, Bill's greatest passion then, and throughout his life, was fishing. We spent hours on the edge of the Coralville Reservoir or the banks of the Iowa River. We bought lures and bait at Cliff Hoag's tackle shop, where Cliff kept a large spoon-billed paddlefish in a tank. When we bemoaned our lack of catches, Cliff alternated explanations: "The water's too warm" or "The water's too cold," phrases Bill and I used for years to explain what we couldn't understand.

After a year and a decision not to pursue a PhD, Bill left Iowa to return to teaching at the University of Missouri. I visited him in Columbia a few times, and he came back to Iowa City to visit me, sampling the homemade saki a number of us were fermenting, and sleeping on the sofa.

When an opening for a poet came up in my department at Fairleigh Dickinson, I encouraged Bill to apply and accept the offer. Several years later, he housesat and cared for our dog when I spent six months in England during my first sabbatical. The next fall, when he was in Spain on his, my family and I visited him in Deja, Mallorca over the Christmas holidays. He introduced me to Robert Graves, drove us around the island in a chartreuse Fiat, helped my young daughters create a tree from scraps, and took us to a village restaurant to introduce me to squid, while his dog, Lady Brett Ashley, slept under the table.

Locals couldn't understand why he had brought a mixed-breed hound all the way from the States, often asking him in their puzzlement if she were a valuable animal. He flew Brett many places over the years, from coast to coast several times. She was a tranquil flyer until some baggage handler misdirected her to Duluth, and she waited several days before being reunited with Bill. From then on, she had to be tranquillized.

Brett didn't come to the upstate New York wedding of one of Bill's former students. Bill was the best man. I was there too, unaware that among the various introductions Bill met Alex, who would become his wife for the next-almost forty years. They hit it off at first sight. When reporting the wedding, the local paper identified the best man as Willard Zarder. Bill loved it, referring to himself by that alter ego again and again.

Bill liked to take long hikes in the woods with Brett and subsequent pet dogs, seeking flights of raptors and spending days on wilderness trails. In his final years, he lived on a lake, splitting logs for a wood stove and taking a boat on the water for fishing. He wrote naturalist articles for magazines in addition to poems, devoting himself to thorough, even meticulous, research — always a stickler for the right detail.

He and I often fished together, travelling the state for lakes and streams. He always caught more than I did. We'd stop for a beer afterward, where he would invariably do his imitation of a fictional good old boy, whose yard we had walked through to reach water: "Get offa my property!"

We did more than fishing; we hung out. Once we went to a double feature of Antonioni films — L'Avventura and La Notte. We went to jazz clubs that no longer exist, heard the Dixieland clarinetist Bobby Gordon in Chester and Johnny Hartman in West Paterson. We gave each other gifts of jazz CDs, although Bill was equally expert in country music, Flatt and Scruggs, Ralph Stanley, The Soggy Bottom Boys. (Bill named a group of guitar-playing MFA students The Soggy Liver Boys.)

Just a couple of months before Bill's death, his self-defined, country-punk performing son, Gabriel, sang Bill's song "Does Your Mother Know You're Sleeping with a Hippy?" to raucous cheers in a local bar. Bill had been in the audience, and laughed when he told me about it. That was one of our last phone conversations. He always ended a phone call with a bit. Like, "May the Good Lord take a liking to you."

Yet for all of his wit and antics and for all of the joy he brought others, Bill was a brooder, confronting shadows that he revealed most openly in his poems, often inseparably from the lightness of their manner. In the last group of poems he wrote, there were a number titled with old sayings, like "Leaving Little to Chance" and "What Do You Want for Nothing?" The concept could have been the source of humor, but Bill probed the veiled potential of the clichés, undermined the seeming obviousness of the colloquial. Life, as explored in these poems, yields much more density and uncertainty, the threat of dark loss. That's seen, for example, in the final lines of "Beyond Belief":

Beyond belief is you, yes, the middle
Of nowhere, almost at home there, too, as if
You had built it, though you can't help looking back
To the place you longed to leave.
              Beyond belief
There is a roaring torrent. It is what is,
Your life, the dream of water going elsewhere.

Whenever I read one of Bill's poems, I can hear his voice, timbre, and rhythm. I am aware of the many references, feel the existential tangles. The poems possess a depth far beyond the surface of the man I knew.

Like so many others, I will miss him very much, perhaps more so because we shared so much in our lives, memories now left only to me.

Note: This essay first appeared in the Spring 2019 issue of *The Literary Review* as part of a tribute to a man who had been a long-time poetry reader for the magazine.

Alison Cummins

When we were engaged, Walter told me I would be meeting his BFF, Bill, a colleague, a journalist, a poet. A poet? I was familiar with teachers and journalists — but a poet? I broke into a sweat.

On the big day, sitting in front of a wood-burning stove, Bill informed me he had worn his best boots for the occasion — tall, unstructured, suede. I remember thinking at the time, "This guy's a poet?"

For some reason I had imaged a self-absorbed, condescending, judgmental man, speaking in iambic pentameter. Bill was none of that.

It's been forty years since that first day, and I'm ashamed to say that although I was aware of Bill's many talents, I thought of him more as husband of Alex, father of boys, and my zany friend.

Only when preparing this book with Walt did I realize the depth and breadth of Bill's intelligence and immense talent. Seeing it come together in one place stunned me.

I'll remember you for many reasons, dear Bill, but most of all for being tall, unstructured, and deep. Very deep.

Pamela Cummins

I have many memories of Uncle Bill, yet the one that stands out was at his retirement party. His party was held at my parents' home (Alison and Walter Cummins) on a beautiful day. I can still picture us by the outside enclosed porch, where I asked him, "So, are you going to do what my so-called retired father does, and still work during your retirement?"

He laughed and replied, "No way! I'm going fishing!"

Which he did for many years. In my mind's eye, I can see him in the afterlife standing at the edge of a gigantic beautiful lake, he's wearing a fisherman's outfit, while swinging his rod backwards in fly fishing style and casting it out into the water. Uncle Bill, fish on …

Jennifer Cummins Grassi

I have a few memories of Uncle Bill. The first going for long walks with my dog Lady and his dog Brett all around our neighborhood near Wetmore Avenue.

I also remember the time I returned from England after being abroad for six months and found him sleeping in my bedroom and was quite upset at the age of eight. He apologized and explained he liked my room best. I guess he liked the color purple because it was everywhere rug, walls and carpet.

When I was a young teenager, he invited us to his home on the lake for a barbecue. We had a fun time. I mostly remember his dog. He said that he had found her on the side of the road she had been hit by a car. He said no one stopped to help her and it made him mad. He stopped and took her home. This smart dog knew how to open the screen door by pushing on the handle to go out back. He was fond of that pup.

Another memory was when he was in Spain on sabbatical and he invited my dad and us to stay in his home. That was the first time I had eaten paella; he made it and it was delicious. We also drink sweet sangria that was a treat for a kid. He was always so interesting and fun to be around. Great memories!

Note: Pamela Cummins and Jennifer Cummins Grassi were, as toddlers, the two little girls who — in "A Farewell to Surrealism" — jumped on the poet at an ungodly hour and were welcomed with hugs.

René Steinke

When my son, Porter, was born, Alex knitted him a perfect, tiny woolen cap, and Bill gave him carefully chosen books, among them, *Animal Fare*, which he handed to me with glee, calling it "subversive poetry!" It's a book of poems for children, built on wordplay with animal names. There's a poem about "the anteloop," (a snake crossed with an antelope), the "whysel," a creature that will question you to death, the "grizzly bare" (a bear without clothes), and Bill's favorite, "the mustank," part-mustang, part-skunk: "They gallop by in thunderous herds / And frighten children, men, and birds; / And for their smell there are no words, / When Mustanks are in town."

It's a wildly fun and weird book, and my son found it hilarious! Every time I read it to him, I thought of Bill. So many of my memories of Bill contain a kind of joyful renegade quality like this. Even when he talked to me about going to church, he did it with a nod to how counter to the norm it could be, and since I was a Lutheran, he teased me about Martin Luther being a heretic. He also teased me about being a "former poet," since I'd started writing novels and had given up poetry, which he jokingly called "the higher calling."

When I first joined the faculty at Fairleigh Dickinson, Bill, along with Walter Cummins, were very welcoming, and I will always be grateful for that. I looked forward to my conversations with Bill in the department's hallway — he would pull me aside before a meeting, hand me a book, and say "read this poem," or hanging out in the department office, he'd ask me if I'd ever heard a particular Hank Williams song, or he would just check in to see if I was doing okay.

At one of the MFA residencies, Bill asked if I would read a long poem, "Gone Haywire," he was working on — he wasn't finished with it yet and wanted to talk it through. I remember being thrilled and touched at his request. I don't think I helped him at all, but it was still a pleasure to look, for just a little while, through the lens he used to see language. Bill was an unusual and wonderful poet, and an unusually kind and wonderful friend.

Renée Ashley

I'd like to begin with the "Introduction" I wrote for Bill's chap-book, *Winter Trees and Other Poems.*

*

Even long before William Zander's poems were written, Robert Frost is said to have stated, "A poem begins in delight and ends in wisdom." Frost clearly saw Zander coming.

One of my favorite poems in Winter Trees is "Mammals." It begins:

> And God said: Let there be mammals, maybe.
> And there appeared like dustballs in the shadows
> shrews and voles and hedgehogs…

If that isn't delight, then there is no such thing! Dustballs! The catalog that follows is long and hilarious ("…marsupials waddled/ with bags of babies") and then, in a turn that both surprises and makes absolute sense, the poem moves towards what was clearly Zander's point all along:

> … And now the mammal
> looked to the stars, noting its nakedness,
> its germs. It tried to fix itself.
> The snow blew in its eyes. The body muttered,
> grew erect like any predator.

We are of the continuum, he says without saying it. Zander is subtle; he knows his craft. He lets his poems speak; he doesn't tell.

Through Zander's phenomenal images, the outside lives in the inside. No matter the poetic platform — and he is accomplished in many: wit, rhyme, and parody among them — his theme is this: Everything is in us. He has always, it seems, understood that the outdoors, and those natures that go wild there, are ours as well, intrinsically, and a part of those internal natures of human physiology and intelligence, of philosophy, of God, and of human entanglements. Oh, he is fully present in his poems, but his presence is osmotic; the visible world has been absorbed, the nature inside and out is a single nature. In "Autumn," he says

> Oh what a lesson!
> crow's wing,
> caddis fly, a trout
> going up my bloodstream.

Though it is tempting to quote every moment like this just to have it in my mouth and in my ears, I will not—but you'll find amiable figurative leeches! And play on woofers and tweeters! These poems are filled with deliciously funny and powerful moments. I'll leave the rest of them in their harmonious contexts for you discover. I've, no doubt, said too much already.

But I'll close with the final stanza of Zander's title poem, the last poem in this collection, in which he brings the many-textured journey to a close, a passage throughout which his skill has been as great as his embrace has been wide.

> The Mind of God! Now, while it sleeps,
> is the time to look into its mysteries.
> See how stark it is, yet deep.
> How empty. Save for winter trees.

There is no daft tree-hugging here; no meaningless verbal pyrotechnics. No exhibitionist on display. William Zander should be named the Poet Laureate of holism — our world needs more of the richness, good humor, intelligence, and plain good sense of his work. This collection is a step towards remedying our shortfall.

*

I was wholly taken off-guard when Bill invited me to become part of the nascent MFA at FDU—and, of course, I jumped at the chance. His was a trusting and generous inclusion. He was just a sort of marvel: students and faculty alike were drawn to him, his easy, everyone-on-the-same-level way of approaching both the work and those he worked with. He made everyone feel welcome from the get-go and he was both funny and irreverent (and I loved so much his irreverence), and, still, I never heard him say an unkind word about anyone. It seems to me, too, that he was a catalyst for decency in others, his easy laughter and his attitude of we're-all-in-this-together created the sweetest context for everyone who was lucky enough to spend time with him. He was generous in the poetry scene, where I met him, and he was generous in his own remarkable poems. You can hear his energies, those of his principles, of his awarenesses, his enthusiasms and loves, embodied in all in those "trout/going up [his] bloodstream." He will be greatly missed. I want to say, again, that "his skill has been as great as his embrace has been wide." I am enlarged by having known him; I have the memories of his friendship and some artefacts of his life: his songs and poetry and art, along with the presence of his family and community, the many, many friends he made while he was here among us. We'll try hard to enact the goodness he taught us ("Oh what a lesson!"), to remember the sweet good he's left behind, the kind of good that we will aspire to and try to build on.

Harry Keyishian

Bill and I had adjoining offices in Hennessy Hall for some years. Across the hall, but down a bit, was the office of Andonis Decavalles. It was a living Poet's Corner for sure. Each would sally forth into the hall in recital mode. I was especially taken by Bill's recitations of Keats, on his way to the department office — "My heart aches, and a drowsy numbness pains my sense as though of hemlock I had drunk" — in his Nebraska accent. I can't, since, think of Keats spoken any other way.

I remember Bill as a passionate union man. The rest of us would wear our union badges when required, and doff them when not, but Bill made his badge a permanent part of his wardrobe. So far as the tedium of department meetings went, Bill was less committed — but we had the benefit of his wonderful caricatures as he wiled away the time.

We tended Bill's dog Lady Brett Ashley for a while when he traveled. She put up with us and was even content — or seemed so. But when Bill walked in the front door, Lady Brett performed an astonishing feat. In a leap she popped into his arms — he didn't have the chance to bend over: she was just there, levitated.

Wanting to keep me current in my areas of scholarship, he once wrote, "Harry — Since you believe that all of Shakespeare's works were really written by Saladin the Saracen, I thought you might enjoy reading 'Wouldn't It Be Cool if Shakespeare Wasn't Shakespeare?' by Stephen Marche in last Sunday's *New York Times Magazine* (Oct. 23). But you probably have. Selah. Onward & upward, Bill Z." Scandalized, I retorted that I was "too busy working on an article proving that Prince Albert wrote all of Dickens and that Jane Austen had a love child with Lord Byron."

Marilyn Rye

It is sad news about Bill Zander, though. He was one of the nicest people in the department and helped me a lot when I started teaching. I was scheduled to teach Advanced Writing, a course I had never taught. Bill shared his syllabus and went into some detail about how he introduced students to the material. The text was Hall's collection of essays by contemporary writers and it was clear from our discussion that Bill wanted students to read a wide range of essays that would help students find their own voices as writers.

One spring day he confided to me that he was missing a department meeting because he was going fishing in a favorite spot in NY (or PA?). The fish were running and Bill's priorities for that day were clear. The amusement in his voice suggested that his plan to miss the meeting added to his adventure. I thought of Bill fishing as I sat through that meeting and couldn't help being amused as well. Bill had the right attitude--there are many routine meeting days but not so many for good fishing.

Geoffrey Weinman

When I arrived at Fairleigh Dickinson in the fall of 1968, I had
the opportunity to meet a group of outstanding faculty in what
was then called the English Department. A number of them be-
came good friends and still are.

Most of the faculty pretty much fit the traditional mode.
Scholarly, bearded, jackets and ties, teaching most of the courses
one would expect an English major to take. But then there was
Bill Zander, with his cap and his lanky stride and his seemingly
casual outlook on the work at hand. I hadn't really known anyone
like him before, and I couldn't quite figure him out. While most
of the faculty were not only engaged in their teaching and schol-
arship, they were also very involved in department, college, and
university politics. Not Bill. He had no time for that. It took me
a very long time to understand that Bill represented the best of
what a faculty member could be — in love with the art of creation
and able to transfer the world of nature with which he surround-
ed himself when away from the institution into the world of his
poetry.

He was a complete person — all the parts fitting together to
create a consistent and beautiful whole. I continue to aspire to be
more like him.

Martin Green

I met Bill Z. when we both joined the English faculty at Fairleigh Dickinson University's Madison campus in the fall of 1966. Walter Cummins, his friend from the Iowa Writers Workshop, recruited Bill to teach journalism, and I was a last minute addition to the faculty on what I thought would be a temporary hiatus from graduate school to replace the department's Chaucer specialist on sabbatical. (In those days, hiring was a lot more casual than today, where positions are posted months in advance of the new academic year and candidates are vetted through MLA interviews, on-campus all-day interviews, and formal presentations). I don't recall when Bill and I started to bond over our mutual love of country and folk music but it must have been soon after we started the school year. I recall several nights in that long-ago autumn when I would stay after classes and Bill and I would go to the Community Bar and Grill or Cutter's in Morristown for a few beers and food and then go to his bachelor pad and play guitar and sing until late in the evening. I was introduced then to Bill's wry wit as a songwriter and also his appreciation of good ol' country tunes. I have a picture in my photo album of Bill and me playing a duet together at a department picnic at Walter Cummins' house early in the summer of '68. We both look so serious — and so young.

Bill's Midwestern plain-folks exterior hid a very sophisticated sensibility, as his poetry demonstrates. He could expound on the modernists with great insight and at the same time he could spin verse tall tales in the voice of his alter ego Hogg Warner. He was attuned to contemporary trends as well. In the wake of a collectively-written popular novel, *Naked Came a Stranger*, Bill and Walter Cummins began a collective novel, *The Peabodys*, which circulated around the department for several months becoming more and more baroque as it passed through many hands. I recall an evening when Bill and Walter and a few other newer faculty members came in to Manhattan (where I was living) and met my wife and me for dinner and drinks with Bill's friends Pat and Elizabeth Crow somewhere in midtown. Pat was working as an editor at the *New Yorker* magazine and he and Bill had a great time reminiscing about days in the Midwest and sharing stories of the writers they knew, which impressed me no end.

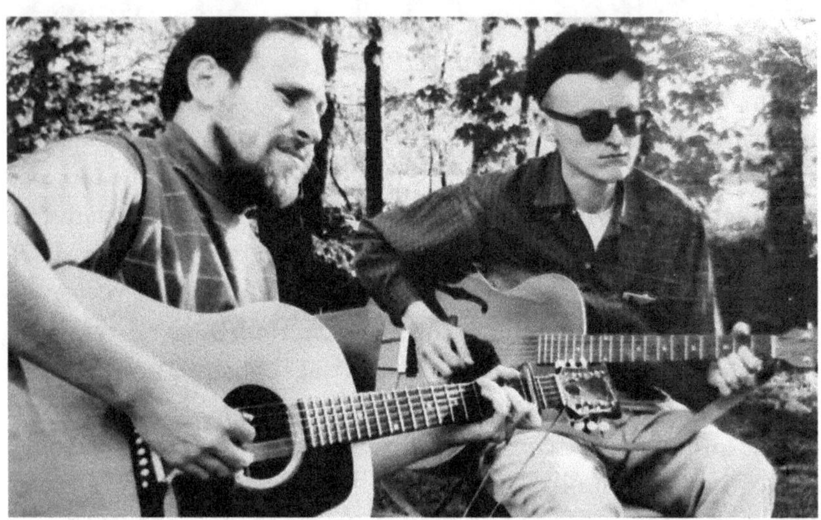

Many years after what began for me as a temporary job had turned into a permanent position I became department chair and Bill became my go-to note taker for meetings. His identification of department members by initials in the minutes (MG, BZ, HK, WC, etc.) became a continuing motif in our department life and his wry commentary enlivened what would otherwise have been routine academic proceedings. He also captured our department doings in witty sketches. I recall one he did (alas, I no longer have it!) of a particularly heated department debate (heated debates were actually a rarity in our department): it showed me as chair tearing my hair (what little I had left by then) surrounded by caricatures of my battling colleagues with me exclaiming, in my best Anglo-Saxon, "Hwaet!" to get their attention.

As Bill and I aged we spent less time together than we had as new faculty friends. Bill married Alex and moved out to a town near the Delaware Water Gap, an hour west of Madison, where they raised their two sons; I continued to live in New York, an hour east of Madison, so social time was limited to department get-togethers. But we worked together for over four decades and I always valued his down-to-earth sense of what our department's mission was: to educate students who could go out to the world with good writing and intellectual skills. In addition to his responsibility for teaching poetry writing—until the inception of the department's full-fledged writing major and MFA in the early 2000s, Bill was our department's main poetry writing teacher — Bill taught journalism, which assumed more importance after the department decided to become a Literature and Communications department. He also developed the Advanced Writing Workshop that we required of all our Communications and writing majors at the time. He handled all these courses, along with some responsibilities in the university's Core Curriculum and an occasional course in Modern Poetry, with his characteristic good grace, humor, and down-to-earth quality.

Martin Donoff

We were sitting in the Georgetown Colonial Malaysian Restaurant waiting for our first course when the lights went out.

Earlier that afternoon Bill, Walt Cummins and I had meandered through Stratford-on-Avon — stopping at places on Sheep Street and then on to Shakespeare's birthplace. We were on a half-day break from the MFA residency and had come to Stratford with some of our students to see a performance by the Royal Shakespeare Company. Bill was his usual amiable self, offering a few of what I thought of as Bill-isms — slightly off-kilter observations that loitered between oddly wry and laugh out loud.

Now, with the power out and the restaurant lit solely by votive candles, our waiter told us that we'd need to reconsider our menu choices. Bill, who had not commented on my peculiar choice of a Malaysian restaurant in Stratford-on Avon, now had to select from dishes more exotic than the ones he had ordered. After a few moments, he looked up at me and offered what would turn out to be his second-best Bill-ism of the night, "What are you going to take us for next — Sumerian food?"

After dinner, with the RSC performance cancelled, we found our students at the bar of the Arden Hotel, one of the few places in town that still had electricity. Bill joined some of the poets at the far side of the bar and I saw them laughing. Probably discussing Sumerian recipes.

Later, on the bus back to our campus at Wroxton, one of the students began reading from a book he'd bought at Shakespeare's birthplace — a collection of poems by Mary Hornby, an early 19th century tenant of the house and a poet who specialized in doggerel.

From the seat behind me, Bill remarked that her poetry was not nearly as bad as that of William McGonagall, often considered the worst poet ever in England. Then, he mused aloud about what an editor might have responded to a submission from Mrs.

Hornby. It was the best Bill-ism of the evening and is indelible in my memory of Bill. "Madam, were it not for William McGonagall, you would be the worst poet in England."

Steve Cameron

Walter Cummins introduced Bill Zander to me during my first year at FDU. For me, always in awe of writers, especially poets, Bill was on the quiet side, though we were often in the same group at lunch and meetings. Walking back to our offices together one morning, we were talking about Iowa, why he wrote poetry, and how ideas occurred to him (wanted to understand what attracted my seven-year-old son, Alex, to be so constantly engaged in reading/writing poems — even at that age, Alex wrote upwards of a dozen poems weekly — many half a page length or longer). At one point, Bill stopped, turned to me, and asked me bring a number of Alex's writings to him. He returned them to me a few weeks later accompanied by a page-long, handwritten note, addressed directly to Alex. It's difficult to accurately describe the exact tenor or Bill's encouragement of young Alex, without entirely reproducing it here. It was kind, thoughtful, not condescending, and surprisingly revealed absolutely no evidence of the amazing disparity in their ages. Bill seemed to address and speak with Alex, as if he were a fellow poet. There were questions for Alex to ponder, ideas for appropriate poetry series, some minor suggestions for Alex to consider — but in general, the gentle praise and reassurance from a comrade. Bill's letter certainly made me envy Bill's university students: tender touch, caring manner, expert ability, view toward his charge's future — everything we all desire in a teacher.

Bob Evans

Bill Zander led the very first poetry session at the very first residency of FDU's MFA program. Though I felt uncomfortable seated there with a bunch of strangers — several of whom have since become my dearest friends — Bill's easygoing manner and light-hearted humor immediately put me at ease. That is until he asked this question: What poet that others hold in high regard do you not particularly care for?

It seemed like a strange question at the time, and to this day I can't remember the reason he asked it. But I thought, what the hell? No one's going to judge anyone here in this kind man's classroom. I girded my loins and volunteered to be the first to speak.

"Wallace Stevens," I said.

I can still remember the vacuum created from the collective gasps of everyone in that room, including Bill. I felt like a grade schooler who had blurted out a profanity to his third grade class at Catholic school (I also have first hand experience in that scenario).

And now, a confession: I still stand by my opinion of Wallace Stevens, so much so that I published a poem several years ago titled "Wallace Stevens Speaks to Me in My Dreams (Because He Doesn't Speak to Me on the Page)". Nevertheless, I continue to pursue the poetry of Stevens to this day, and sometimes my grasp is at least equal to my reach. I doubt this curiosity over a poet whose work at times seems airtight and off limits to my understanding would have persisted beyond that first class had Bill not asked that reverberating question.

Bill and I sometimes spoke together of one of our shared passions: old-time, bluegrass, and gospel music. At one whiskey-fueled, late night wang dang doodle we students were pitching in the dorms, one of us (Bill or me, I'm unsure which) christened the "geezers" of the first MFA cohort "The Soggy Liver Boys" after the Soggy Bottom Boys popularized by the film *O Brother, Where Art Thou?* As one might imagine, the name stuck.

On another occasion, Bill was holding forth on the subject of a certain old-time gospel song by the Stanley Brothers, "Angel Band." Eyes filled with an Old Testament prophet's fire, Bill pulled me aside and said, "It's all in that one word: 'the noise of wings.' We expect to hear 'the sound of wings,' but they sing 'the noise of wings.' Do you hear the difference?"

I heard, so clearly that I titled the only short story I wrote as part of the MFA experience "The Noise of Wings." Thanks to Bill's inspiration and Walter Cummins's thoughtful guidance in the fiction module, it remains the only fiction I've published since the MFA, in a standalone "dime novel" format, the dedication of which reads,

> For Bill Zander,
> Who taught me the importance of noise,
> And Walter Cummins,
> Who helped me find dark music within it.

I'm still chasing after Wallace Stevens, trying to set myself right, and every now and then I hear the Angel Band and its noise of wings. If I had to guess, I'd say I know whose wings are making that noise now.

Mark Hillinghouse

A group of us went to visit Bill during an MFA residency when he was in Kessler for rehab after a car accident. We had all just gotten our tee shirts from Kevin Carey who had printed the words "This Time It's Terminal" on the back as an MFA joke since Kevin was so enamored of the fact that the MFA was a terminal degree. Forgetting what was printed on the backs of our tee shirts a group of five of us walk into Kessler. As we enter the lobby, the staff and the nurses, and other visitors start staring at us in disbelief mouths open wide. Bill got a kick out of this and a good laugh, which is what he needed.

Bill was so happy to see us and he missed being able to participate in the workshops that he taught because he was someone who loved sharing his passion for the craft of writing poetry. And we all missed him. He was the kind of teacher you never forget because he made a lasting impression with his wit and his charm and his acumen and commitment to learning.

*

It was my first time in the Mansion ground floor student snack bar and I was on line for coffee at the machine. Bill who was in front of me wearing his big grin turned to me saying, "Try the Irish Coffee blend, it tastes like it has whiskey!" I grabbed a cup and took a sip and nodded at Bill and told him — it does taste like it has whiskey! Thank you!

Kevin Carey

A Poet After All
For Bill Zander
I was a fiction writer
MFA student, who
took Bill Zander's
poetry module —
the wise cracking
fly fishing poet
who loved to call
us older guys
the soggy liver boys
(a phrase coined by RG Evans)
because we partied
too late in the dorms.
He was droll and witty
and quick to laugh
even when we wore our
This Time Its Terminal shirts
into the rehab to visit him.
But beyond the many
laughs we shared in those
summer Madison moments
what I'll always be grateful for,
until we're both casting in
the same stream someday,
is the boost he gave to
this would be fiction writer,
this uncertain poet who
only began to find a voice
after his simple words
about that first workshopped poem.
"This one's a keeper," he said.
And I believed it.

Jeffrey Triggs

This year we had a sudden snow storm that cost me over four hours getting home from Rutgers. It reminded me of an event in January 1988. I was just starting my first (and only) class teaching at Montclair State. About halfway through the class the students pointed to the window, and I realized that it was starting to snow heavily. I decided to cancel the rest of the class and packed up to head home, but it was already too late. The ride on the Parkway was miserable. All the signs were coated with snow, and the roadways and exits were all coated. I wasn't even sure which exit to take. 78 was just as bad. What should have taken half an hour wound up taking 3 1/2 hours of anxious driving. When I got home, however, I was delighted and surprised to find Bill waiting at my house with Sara and five-year-old Charlotte. He'd apparently be caught by surprise as well at Fairleigh, and thought better of trying to make it back home himself. Since I lived very near Fairleigh, he'd stopped by to see if he could spend the night with us. The "party" was already started when I arrived, and wound up including a lovely dinner with plenty of wine, good conversation, and music. In the morning, Bill helped us shovel out what must have been at least two feet of snow. We made an arrangement that Bill would always be welcome under similar circumstances, and I believe he may have taken us up on it once or twice in the future, but those memories blur and fade with normality in comparison with the drama and delight of the first.

Acknowedgments

Poems by William Zander appeared in the following magazines.

The Apalachee Quarterly
The Beloit Poetry Journal
Berkley Poets Cooperative
Bleb
Blue Unicorn
The Chattahoochee Review
Connecticut Review
Crazy Horse
Dakota Territory
Defined Providence
Descant
Georgetown Review
Hanging Loose
Huron Review
kayak
Light: A Quarterly of Light Verse
Loon
The Louisville Review
Mandrona
Naugahyde Literary Journal
New Letters
The New York Quarterly
Nimrod International Journal of Prose and Poetry
The Pawn Review
Poetry Northwest
Prairie Schooner
Road Apple Review
Slant: A Journal of Poetry
Song
South Dakota Review
Writers Forum
Yankee
Cottonwood Review for the short story, "The Praise of Folly"

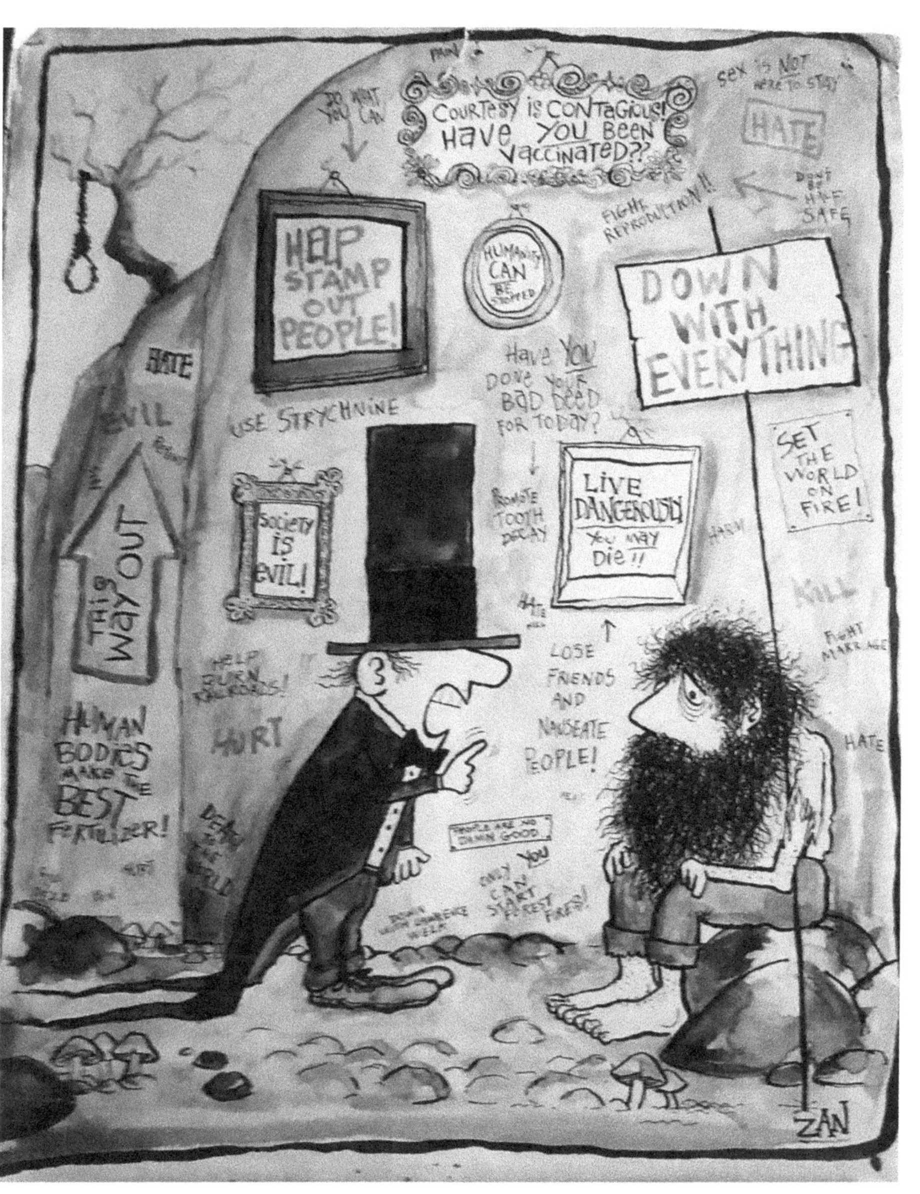

DO WHAT YOU CAN
COURTESY IS CONTAGIOUS! HAVE YOU BEEN VACCINATED??
SEX IS NOT HERE TO STAY
HATE
DON'T BE HALF SAFE
FIGHT REPRODUCTION!!
HELP STAMP OUT PEOPLE!
HUMANITY CAN BE STOPPED
DOWN WITH EVERYTHING
HATE
EVIL
USE STRYCHNINE
Have YOU DONE YOUR BAD DEED FOR TODAY?
PROMOTE TOOTH DECAY
LIVE DANGEROUSLY YOU MAY DIE!!
SET THE WORLD ON FIRE!
Society IS EVIL!
THIS WAY OUT
HELP BURN RAILROADS!
HURT
HARM
KILL
LOSE FRIENDS AND NAUSEATE PEOPLE!
FIGHT MARRIAGE
HATE
HUMAN BODIES MAKE THE BEST FERTILIZER!
PEOPLE ARE NO DAMN GOOD.
ONLY YOU CAN START FOREST FIRES!
ZAN